AWESO ODESA

Interesting things you need to know

2nd edition

Kyiv
Osnovy Publishing
2019

УДК 908(477.74-25)(036)=111
О-41

Authors of Awesome Ukraine series — Hanna Kopylova, Dana Pavlychko
Executive Editor — Nadia Chervinska
Authors of texts — Igor Makhtiienko, Victoria Linchevskaya
English editor — Daisy Gibbons
Cover illustration — Zukentiy Gorobiyov
Design and layout — Dmytro Ermolov, Kateryna Smoliarova
Photo Editor — Anna Lysiuk

Printing — Publish Pro, www.publishpro.com.ua

Osnovy Publishing
osnovypublishing@gmail.com
www.osnovypublishing.com

ISBN 978-966-500-840-8

FOREWORD

Odesa — the "pearl of the Black Sea" — is a vibrant, multicultural port city. Its quirky architecture and laid-back beach culture have long made it a popular spot for tourists, and an inspiration for writers. Its vibrant streets, good music, eclectic food, and live theater entice visitors to come and unwind.

Odesa is open to the world. Since its founding, the city has had mayors of Spanish, Greek, and French origin, and its planners and architects have hailed from Italy, France, Germany, and the Netherlands. Their cultural influences along with the native Tatar, Ukrainian, Russian, and Jewish populations resulted in an atmosphere of diversity and inclusivity.

With this book, we are pleased to share with you our love for Odesa! The book is neither a guide nor a manual. Rather, it's an insight into the city we adore — mellow, eclectic, and seductive. On its pages you'll find references to major historical events, famous and talented residents, art, culture, sports, literature, traditions, and even the best street food.

CONTENTS

HISTORY

Right page: Thomas Lawrence, **Armand Emmanuel Duc of Richelieu**, *1818*

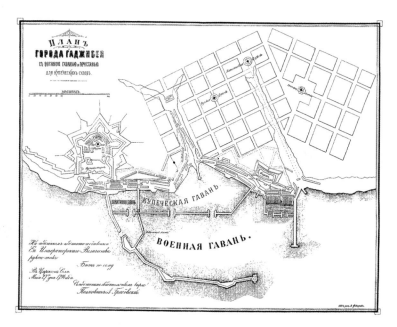

Khadzhibei

Records of this settlement date back to antiquity

In the 14th century, the Genoese settlement Ginestra, which was the anchorage point for merchant vessels, appeared on the map. After the Tatars seized the land in the 15th century, the first information about the future Khadzhibei / Kochubei settlement appeared. However, the settlement was soon destroyed and was only rebuilt 200 years later by the Ottoman Empire. In 1765, the Turks seized and strengthened the abandoned fort, calling it Yeni Dunya. Next to the stone castle a Turkish settlement called Khadzhibei appeared. At that time, it was home to Tatars,

Petr Parkhet, **Conquest of Khadzhibey Fortress,** 1954

There are several versions of the origin of the name Khadzhibei. According to one, the Tatar fortress was named after *a Tatar bey (chieftan) called Hadji*. But most believe that the name is from the word for sacred pilgrimage, the hajj, to Mecca Odesa's first mayor and founder Jose de Ribas received *the Order of St. George's of the Third Degree* for the capture of Khadzhibei. With a small detachment of Cossacks, he quickly and unexpectedly took the fortress, with virtually no losses, and captured Ahmed Pasha

Turks, and Greeks. Even then, multi-ethnicity was one of the features of the future city of Odesa.

During the Russo-Turkish war, Khadzhibei was taken by a small detachment of Odesa's future founder, José de Ribas. The fortress was destroyed and the first wharf of the Odesa Port was built in its place. The location of the fortress was ideal for the creation of a military and commercial port. An estuary on the outskirts of Odesa was named after the fortress. It was also a popular health resort in the 19th and early 20th centuries.

Catherine II of Russia

It was the odious ruler of the Russian Empire
who ordered the construction of the Odesa port

Settlements on the territory of modern Odesa have existed since antiquity.
The Genoese, Turks, Greeks, and Tatars all have a connection to Odesa. But
the city in its modern form appeared only upon the decree of Catherine
II to construct a port on the site of the former Khadzhibei fortress. She
believed it was an excellent location, which could be used advantageously
during wars.

On May 27, 1794, Catherine II issued an edict to begin construction of
the settlement and port. She sent Spanish citizen José de Ribas to Odesa as
a guide, and he subsequently became Odesa's first mayor. Together with
Franz de Volán, who developed the construction plan, de Ribas proceeded to
manage the masonry works. At the same time, it was decided to name the
new city Odesa, in honour of the Greek colony of Odesos, which had once
existed nearby.

Catherine II was known to have many lovers, and one of her favorites was Grigory Potemkin. *The Potemkin Steps* were named after him, and a sculpture of him adorns a monument to the founders of Odesa

Catherine II's son, *Emperor Pavel I*, was not so sympathetic towards Odesa and even rescinded all funding of the city's development. There is a well-known story about how Odesans managed to change his mind by sending him *a crate of oranges*. A monument to the oranges is located on *Zhvanetskyi Boulevard*

Top: Monument to **Catherine II of Russia** on Katerynynska Square
Left page: George Christopher Grooth, **Portrait of Tsarevich Peter Fedorovich and Grand Princess Ekaterina Alexeevna**, 18th century

In honour of the city's hundred-year anniversary, in 1900 the citizens of Odesa decided to establish a monument to the empress as the founder of their city. This monument was erected on Katerynynska Square.

José de Ribas

Odesa's central street, Derybasivska Street, is named in honour of José de Ribas, the city's founder and first mayor

José de Ribas was a Spanish nobleman born in Naples. At the age of 18 he joined the Russian Imperial Army. Participation in Russo-Turkish wars and the storming of Izmail brought him fame and many awards; Lord Byron even mentioned de Ribas's military exploits in the book *Don Juan*.

On September 2, 1794, José de Ribas built several wharfs and a couple of churches on the site of the Khadzhibei Ottoman garrison town. This date became recognized as the date of the founding of Odesa. The city was one of the few at the time that were built and developed according to a pre-approved plan. This plan was created by de Ribas and Dutch engineer Franz de Volan. As a result, the historic center is divided into rectangular blocks with well-defined squares and main streets.

The development of the port was a key factor in Odesa's rapid development. The city quickly began to expand, attracting a large number of new residents. Within 3 years, de Ribas had laid the foundations for the further transformation of Odesa into the biggest center south of the Russian Empire.

One of de Ribas's brothers, Felix, also lived in Odesa. *The Odesa City Garden* was established due to his efforts. His house was located there, but did not survive in its original form

Derybasivska Street is only 3 *blocks long*, but this has not prevented it from becoming one of the most popular streets for city residents and tourists

Left page; Johann Baptist von Lampi the Elder, **Portrait of Admiral Osip Mikhailovich de Ribas**, *1796*

Duc de Richelieu

The great-great-great-nephew of Cardinal Richelieu from Alexandre Dumas's book The Three Musketeers and one of the founding fathers of Odesa

French nobleman Armand-Emmanuel Sophie-Septimanie Vignerot du Plessis was enlisted by Duc de Richelieu in the Russian Imperial Army during the French Revolution. He won favors at the court of the Russian tsar Alexander I, who appointed him to govern Odesa.

Richelieu became the mayor of Odesa in 1803, a post he held for almost 11 years. He laid many of the streets and avenues of the city center. He established special economic benefits that made the city attractive to traders from all countries. During Richelieu's tenure as mayor of Odesa the city's population increased threefold.

It was under his leadership that Odesa became the city of acacias. Having bought acacia seedlings with his personal funds, the count distributed them free of charge to anyone interested. Richelieu also paid much attention to education, establishing several schools. In 1817, an institution that he had created was transformed into a lyceum. Later it

There is a plaque on the Richelieu monument which still has *chips and holes* in it, received during the Crimean war and from the bombing of the city by a British squadron. On the back of the statue are *traces of bullets*. The pedestal was also damaged, but it was patched up after the war

Top: Statue of the **Duc de Richelieu** on Prymorskyi Boulevard, 7
Left page: Thomas Lawrence, **Armand Emmanuel Duc de Richelieu**, 1818

was named after him; to this day it is known as the most prestigious school in Odesa. After his tenure as Odesa mayor, he twice held the post of prime minister of France.

Six years after his death, a bronze monument was erected in his honour that became the city's trademark.

5

Porto Franco

The Italian term porto franco (free port) played a key role in transforming Odesa into a great trade and cultural city

Odesa received this status in 1819, thanks to mayor Armand-Emmanuel du Plessis de Richelieu and his successor count Alexandre Langeron. That determined the vector of the city's development for the next 40 years.

Odesa was the southern trading center of the Russian Empire and one of the fastest growing cities in Europe. In terms of population, Odesa was fourth after St. Petersburg, Moscow and Warsaw at that time.

The border of the free port area was held at what is currently Staro-portofrankivskyi Street. There are no buildings on the even side of the street, as there used to be a 25 kilometer ditch there. Customs checkpoints were established at some spots. But the city's rapid growth caused it to lose its status as a duty-free port. Odesa had become too large and wealthy, and the presence of the border only hindered its development. There were too many goods, and that gave rise to smuggling at customs. The status was annulled in 1859, allowing the city to expand and focus on its own production of goods.

Due to the large flow of contraband goods, the construction of residential houses on the odd side of the current *Staroportofrankovskyi Street* was banned. This was due to the fact that houses could easily store contraband goods. Therefore, only government agencies could be built there

According to memoirs from those years, the salaries of drivers and freight workers were very high due to the huge turnover of goods. Sometimes so high that they would use small bills to light cigarettes and tobacco. At that time the export of grain from Odesa was larger than all US ports combined

Lustdorf

This colony near Odesa was founded by immigrants from Southern Germany in 1805 when Odesa was a steadily-growing city

Initially, the settlement was called Kaiserheim. According to the legend, Odesa mayor Richelieu visited the colony and liked its character, which prompted the name to be changed to Lustdorf, which means "merry village" in German. Lustdorf was a typical German settlement with a marketplace, church and city hall; it grew and developed quickly.

Besides Lustdorf, there was an extensive network of other German colonies near Odesa. The largest of them was called *Gross-Liebenthal*, which means "valley of great love." The settlement was famous for its wine production. The colony's name was later changed to Mariinskyi, and is now called Velykodolyns'ke. A new brand of wine called Gross-Libenthal is currently being produced here

At the end of the 19th century, *a British Indo-European telegraph line* was established connecting London and Calcutta. The telegraph line passed through many countries of the world, and one of the points was Lustdorf, where a telegraph station was built. The line was established in 1870 and lasted until 1931

This remoteness of the German colony and its rapid growth led to the establishment of Odesa's first electric tram line.

In 1881, a steam tram line was established in Odesa, but the last station was Velykyi Fontan. Those going further to Lustdorf had to travel in carts. In 1906, the people of Lustdorf laid a track in order to connect Lustdorf with Velykyi Fontan by electric tram. This made it much easier to travel between Lustdorf and Odesa, and the village became a resort town for Odesa city dwellers.

The present name of the village is Chornomorka. Some old buildings and street names remain from the original settlement. The name Lustdorf was given to a well-known Odesa Brewery.

Hryhoriy Marazli

Marazli held the post of mayor for 17 years. Odesans remember him most for his patronage and love of his city

Hryhoriy Marazli (Grigorios Maraslis) was born on Hretska Street (literally Greek Street) into a wealthy family of Greek origin who came from the current Plovdiv area in Bulgaria. Marazli received a good education in the best educational institution of Odesa, the Richelieu Lyceum.

Instead of continuing his family business, he chose a career in civil service and was elected mayor of Odesa in 1877. During the time he held this position, the city developed considerably. The city park, new tram lines, running water, and the city's first stadium are only some of his achievements. Marazli is known for having built shelters for the homeless and needy with personal funds. This earned him the love and

A street was named after Marazli during his lifetime, in 1895. Most of the plots of land belonged to his family. After becoming mayor, Marazli sold them at a very low price to wealthy and noble families with one condition: that they build attractive looking houses or mansions. This street became one of the most beautiful in Odesa

Top: An ambulance carriage near the first Ambulance Station, which was built on the mayor's means
Left page: Ivan Karchev, **Portrait of Grigorios Maraslis, the Mayor of Odesa,** *1896*

respect of the citizens of Odesa. Many of the buildings he built or owned are still standing today.

Marazli funded the construction of the Russian Empire's first bacteriological institute. He also donated one of his palaces to the city, which now houses the Museum of Fine Arts. Marazli was buried with great honors in the Greek Holy Trinity Church. However, his body was reburied during Soviet times, and the place of his grave is no longer known.

Marazli Street is also linked to *several legends.* One bas-relief on *the building at №54* depicts a woman with a noose around her neck. Some say it was made by the owner in memory of his wife who hanged herself

8

The Greek Revolution

On September 14, 1814, the Filiki Eteria society held their first-ever gathering in Odesa. It marked the beginning of Greece's struggle for independence from the Ottoman Empire

The name Filiki Eteria is translated as Society of Friends. It was a secret society that originally consisted of about 20 close friends united by the idea of an independent Greece. The structure was something similar to the structure of the Masonic lodges. The organization had 4 levels of in-itiation: Brothers or Vlamides, the Recommended, Priests, and Shepherds. At the head was the so-called Invisible Authority, which carried out orders without discussion. Odesa mayor Hryhoriy Marazli was one of the organizers and patrons of the society.

Ξάνθος

Σκουφάς

Τσακάλωφ

The secret society's slogan "*Freedom or death,*" became the symbol of the Greek struggle for independence. The Greek words Ελευθερία ή θάνατος contain 9 syllables, the same as the number of blue stripes on the Greek flag

In 1821, *the Odesa Filiki Eteria Society* was transformed into the Odesa Greek Philanthropic Society. It was created to provide assistance to refugees of Greek origin from the Ottoman Empire. However, despite its focus, the

society continued to function as Filiki Eteria, carrying out a political agenda

Unknown artist, **Alexandros Ypsilanti**

In 1818, representatives of the Greek liberation movement joined the organization and the society's main residence was moved to Constantinople, the capital of the Ottoman Empire. The new leader became Greek national hero Alexandros Ypsilanti. In 1821, he led an uprising against Ottoman rule. After 11 years of conflicts and revolts, Greece achieved independence from the Ottoman Empire.

Today a Greek Cultural Center and the Filiki Eteria museum is located in a building on Odesa's Chervonyi Lane. Thanks to this spot, Odesa will forever be a part in the history of Greece's independence.

9

Chumka Hill

There is an urban legend about hidden treasures at Chumka Hill, the burial mound of those who died from the plague

Odesa was overcome by the plague (chuma) epidemic several times in the 19th century. As in the Middle Ages, the illness was brought by ships that came into the port. The most severe plague outbreak occurred in 1812. After the Russo-Turkish war, merchant ships from the Ottoman Empire began to enter the city en masse, bringing the terrible disease into the city.

    The number of cases was so huge that there were not enough hospital beds. The city announced a strict quarantine, closing all entry points to the city and even the port. Residents were strictly forbidden from appearing on the streets. However, the plague still raged until the end of the year, and the

There is an artificial mountain on *Vodoprovidna street*, under which the victims of the plague epidemic are buried

During plague epidemics, debris was brought to *Chumka Hill* to cover the dead bodies

By the middle of the 19th century, the amount of debris and rubble was so great that the road located near the hill became known popularly as *Rubbish-Strasse*

Later, a water tower was built near the hill along with the first water pipes bringing running water to the city. Since then, the street has been called *Vodoprovodna*, which roughly translates to *aqueduct*

*On the medals, it says, "**For the cessation of plague in Odesa.**"*

number of deaths was enormous. *Mortus* (specially designated people) collected the dead and buried them in a designated cemetery. Later, the cemetery was covered with earth and debris, which became Chumka Hill. In 1829, a stone sign was placed on the spot in memory of the deceased.

Alexander Bernardazzi

It was Bernardazzi who gave Odesa's city center its unique appearance, having designed both private and public buildings

Alexander Bernardazzi was born in Russia in 1831 to a Swiss Italian family. After studying at the St. Petersburg College of Architecture and Construction, Bernardazzi was sent to Bessarabia where he spent 30 years as the chief architect of Chisinau. In 1878, he moved to Odesa.

In Odesa, Bernardazzi initially worked as a lecturer at the Imperial Novorossiya University (later the Odesa National University), and then as the city's chief architect. Bernardazzi's two most notable projects in Odesa's city center are the Hotel Bristol and the New Stock Exchange. They are located across the street from one another on Pushkinska Street and are acknowledged as masterpieces of Odesa architecture.

The Stock Exchange Building now housing the Odesa Philharmonic was built in the image of the Doge's Palace in Venice. Thanks to

A monument to Alexander Bernardazzi was erected during his lifetime in 1900. In honour of *the 50th anniversary of his architectural career*, a marble bust of the architect was unveiled in the the Odesa Philharmonic building

The wine restaurant Bernardazzi is located in the courtyard of the Philharmonic. It has the largest wine list in Ukraine, including more than 1000 different types

the original design, the Philharmonic has excellent acoustics.

In addition, Bernardazzi designed residential buildings, a hospital, the Medical University and a Presbyterian church. He also implemented projects designed by other architects, such as the railway station, housing for the disabled, and the building of the Russian Technical Society.

Ze'ev Jabotinsky

Revisionist Zionist leader, journalist
and translator

Ze'ev Jabotinsky was one of the leaders of right-wing Zionism and the founder of the Zionist Revisionist movement. He campaigned for establishing a Jewish majority in Palestine and for re-establishing the Jewish armed forces.

He was born on October 18, 1880 in Odesa, where he also began his career as a journalist and took an active part in the Zionist movement. He soon became known as a powerful speaker and an influential leader.

Jabotinsky expressed the need to revise Zionism's traditional ideologies, which is why the Revisionist movement was formed under him. He was against socialist ideology, which at the time was integral to the contemporary Zionist movement, arguing instead that class struggle undermined the national unity of the Jews. He was also one of

Top: Jabotinsky (in the center) and Meir Kahane (second right) in Paris

Jabotinsky established several Jewish organizations, including **Beitar** and **HaTzohar**, both based on Revisionist Zionism

He was friends with **Korney Chukovsky**, who said that Jabotinsky helped him at the beginning of his literary career

the founders of the Jewish Legion, which fought alongside the British Army during the First World War.

From 1923, Jabotinsky was editor of the Jewish weekly *Dawn*, published first in Berlin, then in Paris.

Besides his journalistic work, he also wrote novels. His novel *The Five*, written in 1935, contains a lot of poetic descriptions of early-twentieth-century Odesa, with portraits of its streets and characters.

Odesa's Main Synagogue

This synagogue brings together hundreds of worshippers

Odesa's Jewish population has always been fairly sizeable. The city's first synagogue was built back in 1798, and in 1855 a new synagogue — which then became the city's main synagogue — was built by the Italian architect F. Morandi. The facade and the interior of the imposing building designed in the Florentine-Roman style. It is located on the corner of Rishelievska and Yevreiska streets. "Yevreiska Street" translates as "Jewish Street", further demonstrating the city's Jewish heritage.

The building was not always used as a place of worship. In 1919, after the Russian Revolution, the state sequestered the building and took it from the Jewish community for its own use, and it ceased to operate

There were more than 250 synagogues in Odesa *100 years ago*, now there are 3

as a synagogue. At first it was a natural history museum, later being turned into a children's musical theater, and finally, it became a sports hall for a teacher training college.

The building was only returned to the community for use as a synagogue after the Soviet period. In 1996 it was rebuilt, and the building's original features were restored.

Today the synagogue is a religious, cultural and educational center with a wide variety of social services provided to the community. Within the building the Jewish community opened a kindergarten, library and two schools that work on the basis of charity and provide services without any payment. The synagogue also houses a kosher restaurant in the basement.

On holidays and feast days Jews from the Odesa region and all over Ukraine come to pray here

CULTURE

*Right page: Oleksandr Roitburd, **Bird**, 1994*

Kyriak Kostandi

The most prominent of Ukrainian Wandering artists, a member of the Imperial Academy of Arts came from a poor suburb of Odesa

Kostandi was born near Odesa in 1852 to a family of immigrants from Greece. After moving to Odesa, he worked in a photography shop. There, his talent was noticed and he was invited to the Odesa Drawing School. After graduating, he entered the Saint Petersburg Academy of Arts under the patronage of Ivan Aivazovsky. Afterward, he returned to Odesa as a teacher at his former drawing school. Kostandi was the main ideologist of the Peredvizhniki (Wandering) realist painters in the south of Ukraine. He was one of the founders of the Society of South Russian Artists, which he led until the end of his life. In 1900, he became a member of the Saint Petersburg Academy of Arts, and 10 years later he became the director of the Odesa Museum of Art.

Kostandi's talents and his paintings have been recognized by many prominent artists. In 1900, his painting *Early Spring* was awarded a bronze medal at the World Exhibition in Paris.

At the age of 18 he was given the chance to enter *the drawing school* founded by Odesa's mayor Hryhoriy Marazli. His charcoal drawings were accidentally seen by Aivazovsky, who helped get him accepted to the school

The Society of South Russian Artists was founded by Kostandi and other artists in Odesa. The society held exhibitions of the works of Aivazovsky, Serov, Repin, and Levitan. After the death of Kostandi, the organization was renamed *the Society of Kostandi*

Clockwise: Kyriak Kostandi, **Early Spring**, 1915; Kyriak Kostandi; **Geese**, 1913; Kyriak Kostandi, **The Artist's Family**, 1901

His chamber paintings reflect the beauty of the landscapes of Odesa. In his works, nature is not a passive participant but rather the main protagonist; this is achieved through elements of Impressionism. A large collection of Kostandi's paintings are on display at the Odesa Museum of Art.

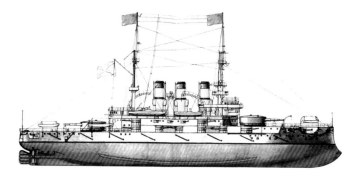

Eisenstein's Battleship Potemkin

This legendary film has been recognized as one of the greatest films of all time

Battleship Potemkin was the hallmark film of Sergei Eistenstein and was shot in Odesa contrary to the original plans. It was fully filmed in black and white, but one of the scenes appears in color. The director came up with the innovative technique of adding color to the negatives by hand. Thus it became the first color film in the USSR. The most famous scene of the film is of a baby in a pram rolling down the Potemkin Steps amidst the chaos of the mutiny. This scene was recreated in several other films, such as *Star Wars: Episode III – The Revenge of the Sith, The Untouchables*, and even in the animated series *The Simpsons*. Eisenstein noted that the idea for this scene came to him as he was eating cherries and watching the pits roll down the steps.

The soundtrack, originally written by Edmund Meisel, was

The film is based on real-life events that occurred in 1905 aboard *the Prince Potemkin Tavrichesky Russian battleship*, in which the crew revolted and seized the ship

The flag seen flying on the ship after the crew had mutinied was white, which is the color of the tsars, but this was done so that it could be *hand-painted red*, which is the color of communism. Since this is a black-and-white film, if the flag had been red it would have shown up black in the film

Clockwise: *Sergei Eisenstein editing the Battleship Potemkin film; Poster for the* **Battleship Potemkin**; *Still frame from the Battleship Potemkin (Goskino USSR);*

reinvented several times. Dmitri Shostakovich, one of the best-known composers of the 20th century, wrote a new soundtrack for the film's 50th anniversary, and in 2007 the band *The Pet Shop Boys* com-posed their version. British mini-malist composer Michael Nyman wrote an alternative soundtrack in 2011, and performed with his orchestra at the Potemkin Steps in 2015.

Ilf and Petrov

Ostap Bender from "The Twelve Chairs" is one of the world's most famous conmen

Ilya Ilf (Ilya Arnoldovich Feinsilberg) was born into the family of an Odesa banker. Ilf tried various professions before eventually becoming a journalist. In 1923, he moved to Moscow, where he met Yevgeny Petrov while working for the newspaper *Gudok*. Unlike Ilf, Yevgeny Petrov was born into a literary family. His older brother Valentin Kataev was a famous Odesan writer. For this reason, Yevgeny took a pseudonym. Petrov worked in the criminal investigation department for several years, which subsequently served as a source of insight in his writing.

In 1927, Ilf and Petrov began writing the novel *The Twelve Chairs*, in which the swindler and "grand strategist" Ostap

Ilf and Petrov were *the first Soviet journalists* that revealed the Great Depression-era America to millions of readers in the USSR

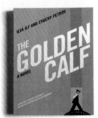

Bender first appeared. The character was so colorful and original that he later became an inspiration for many other writers. Having written the sequel *The Little Golden Calf*, Ilf and Petrov traveled to America. The trip inspired them to write a collection of notes called *Little Golden America*. Ilf contracted tuberculosis during the journey and died upon his return to Odesa. Petrov was a war correspondent during the Second World War, during which he died in a plane crash.

When writing the book *Little Golden America*, Ilf and Petrov crossed USA twice from one end to the other, a journey which took them 3 months

One of the streets in Odesa has been named in honor of the two writers, and the smallest square in the world was named after Ostap Bender. It is located within the Odesa City Garden.

David Oistrakh

The world-renowned violinist David Oistrakh, who owned a Stradivarius violin, was born in Odesa

David Oistrakh began taking an active interest in music at the age of three when his father gave him a toy violin. He also spent a lot of time with his parents in the theater, where he was noticed by well-known music teacher Pyotr Stolyarsky. He later acquired the foundations of music at Stolyarsky music school. Oistrakh then studied at the Odesa Conservatory, graduating in 1926. While still a student, he performed with the Odesa Symphony Orchestra as a conductor and soloist. This was the beginning of his concert career.

The musical works of Serhiy Prokofiev had a major influence on Oistrakh, and he performed Prokofiev's violin concerto for his final examination. In 1928, Oistrakh moved to Moscow. There he quickly rose from a talented provincial musician to one of world fame. In addition to his musical activities, Oistrakh was known as a very good chess player. In 1937, he held a chess match with Serhiy Prokofiev and won.

David Oistrakh, the violin virtuoso, was appreciated as a performer and conductor. His impressive musical talents earned him the nickname "King David."

In 1937, David Oistrakh won the grand prize at *the Queen Elisabeth Competition* in Brussels. In 1937 and 1938 the competition was held under the patronage of Elisabeth of Bavaria, Queen of Belgium. It was this award that brought Oistrakh world fame. She presented Oistrakh with a Stradivarius violin

The famous chess match between *Oistrakh and Prokofiev* took place in Moscow, and according to the regulations, the loser was obliged to give a concert. Though Prokofiev lost, Oistrakh decided to take part in Prokofiev's concert

*Bottom: David Oistrakh in the class of the famous violinist and eminent pedagogue **Petro Stolyarsky***

Isaac Babel

He was a master of "short prose,"
and one of Odesa's favorite writers

Babel was born into a Jewish family in Odesa, in the Moldavanka quarter. At that time it was a poor, troubled and multiethnic area. Moldavanka later appeared as the main setting
for Babel's *Odesa Stories*. Due to the discrimination against Jews
at the time, Babel was denied entry into college upon his first
application. But that did not stop him. His first short stories
were written at the age of 15, in French. In addition, he was
fluent in Yiddish, Russian and Ukrainian.

    Isaac Babel was an astute observer of the Odesan way of
life, which formed the basis for his literary works. One of
the main characters in his book *Odessa Stories* is Benya Krik.
Benya personified the phrase "a Jew is able to fend for himself." Babel's stories were born from a love for his city and

One of Babel's
first short stories,
published in 1916
and entitled Shchel,
almost landed
him in *prison*.
He developed
a scandalous
reputation since
the plot of the
story was based
on the life of
prostitutes.
For this he
was accused
of spreading
pornography.
His court hearing
was only avoided
because of the
February 1917
revolution

In 1921, Babel was assigned to serve in *S. Budyonny's Cavalry Army*, which was stationed on the Polish front. The army consisted of Don Cossacks, whose attitudes toward Jews were hostile. Thus, Babel adopted the pseudonym Kirill Liutov

In his notes, Babel described the unpleasant details of the campaign, including what he called their "red terror". Budyonny's Cossacks looted and raped in Polish villages, massacring the Polish and Jewish populations. All this is described in his book *Red Cavalry*

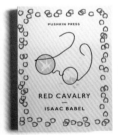

*Top: Isaac Babel with **daughter Liza**, Moscow, 1967*

his childhood memories. His collection of stories called the *Red Cavalry* was the cause of strained relations with the Soviet authorities as it shone light on unpleasant facts that ran counter to official propaganda. Largely due to this collection, Babel was arrested and executed in 1940. His memory is honored by a statue on Richelieu Street.

Emil Gilels

One of the best pianists of the 20th century was born in Odesa

World-famous pianist Emil Gilels was born in Odesa on October 6, 1916, into an intellectual Jewish family. His father was an accountant and his mother was a housewife. He could already play the piano at the age of five. It is unclear whether or not his talent was due to an innate ability or his early start. In 1931, Gilels received a favorable review from the illustrious Arthur Rubinstein. Emil's teacher at the Odesa Conservatory had requested Rubinstein listen to the boy play during one of his visits to Odesa.

Emil first experienced real fame, though, after his victory at the First All-Union Competition of Performers. Not only his victory, but also the audience's reaction, went down in history. One newspaper wrote that after his performance the people cheered, hugged and congratulated one another other on the emergence of a new genius.

This victory was followed by a postgraduate course under the direction of Neuhaus, whose outlook and worldview was a great influence on Gilels's development. Gilels

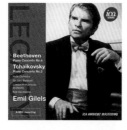
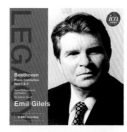

Emil Gilels played a very important role in saving *the Lutheran Church of Odesa.* He used his contacts with the editorial board of *the Pravda and Izvestia* newspapers and, of course, the Ministry of Culture of the USSR, in order to prevent the church from being knocked down

In addition to his other awards, Emil Gilels held such titles as *Honorary Member of the London Royal Academy of Music, Honorary member of the F. Liszt Academy of Music, Honorary member of the Academia di Santa Cecilia,* and awards such as the Order of Merit in Culture and Arts (France), Order of Leopold I (Belgium) and the Gold Medal of the City of Paris, France

received numerous awards one after the other, both Soviet, such as the Stalin Prize of the first degree, and international, such as the Robert Schumann prize. Gilels's technique differed in its depth of content and high technicality, a particular fullness and depth of sound, and its elegance of interpretations and lyricism. During the war, Gilels gave concerts in besieged Leningrad, and afterward went back to giving concerts and teaching.

Interestingly, after his triumphant victory in the first competition in Moscow, the young pianist was asked by Stalin where he would like to live, in Odesa or Moscow. Without hesitation Gilels replied, "In Odesa." However, an eventual move to the USSR capital was necessary for the pianist's career. It was there that he passed away on November 14, 1985.

19

1895–1982
Леонид Утесов
РОССИЯ · ROSSIJA · 1999 2.00

Leonid Utyosov

Utyosov's "At the Black Sea" is considered Odesa's trademark song

The future singer and actor, who was given the name Lazar at birth, grew up in the large family of Jewish merchant Weissbein. Leonid dropped out of school in his teen years and began performing with a circus troupe, and later at the Kremenchuk Theater of Miniatures. In 1921, Utyosov went to Moscow to work in a theater headed by Mayakovsky. It was there that his acting talent was able to blossom to its full potential.

Once, while in Paris, the Odesa native heard an American jazz orchestra and decided to create his own. Later, his orchestra played in the Soviet musical *Jolly Fellows*. It was after that film that Utyosov's success as a musician and actor became widely recognized. Despite the fact that he lived most of his life outside of Odesa, Utyosov retained a love for the city of

The USSR's ruling elite were admirers of *Utyosov's songs*. However, he was forbidden from performing many of them because gangster romance was taboo at the time. Since Stalin liked his songs, Utyosov was not subjected to the same rigid censorship as other performers and artists of the time

On Derybasivska
street there is
a monument
dedicated to the
memory of Leonid
Utyosov

*Clockwise: Leonid Utyosov on the wing of the **La-5F fighter**, that was built on the means from his ensemble*
*"The Merry Fellows"; Leonid Utesov and Lubov Orlova in a comedy **Funny Guys** (Mosfilm, 1934); the album*
cover of CD with Leonid Utyosov songs
Left page: Leonid Utyosov on a Russian postage stamp, 1999

his childhood and adolescence. His songs about Odesa became
an integral part of urban folklore. In the smallest square in
the world, located in the Odesa City Garden, there is a bronze
monument to the singer and actor. And his former apartment
on Utyosov Street has been turned into a museum.

Odesa Philharmonic Theater

The theater was constructed between 1894 and 1898 under the direction of Alexander Bernardazzi

The building was originally constructed to house the New Stock Exchange and was designed in the Venetian Gothic style, with Renaissance elements. In 1924, it became the Odesa Philharmonic. In 1937, under the Soviet government, it was transferred to state ownership. The spacious concert hall with 1,000 seats is considered unique because of its acoustics and visual beauty. When designing the building, Bernardazzi achieved the effect in which the total conductivity of sound was excellent, but the merchants at the time of transactions could not hear what their neighbors were discussing.

The building's walls have heard everything from concerts and balls of Imperial Russia to the Soviet plenums.

There have also been closed-door innovative performances from those by playwright Roman Viktyuk to ones by masters such as Feodor

The wooden ceiling of the Philharmonic's central hall was made from gilded cedar of Lebanon, and constructed without a single nail

They say that the great Hungarian composer and pianist **Franz Liszt** once gave a concert in the Odesa Philharmonic Theater

Chaliapin. It was here that Vladimir Mayakovsky gave his last speech in Odesa.

The main staircase of the Philharmonic is made from Carrara marble. A side niche of the central entrance houses a bust of Bernardazzi. And on either side of it you can read the engraved names of those who worked on the construction of the building: the stone setters, sculptors, woodcarvers, and artists. You can also find there many Masonic symbols, including the compass, square, chisel, hammer, saw, pliers and palette. The ceiling of the main entrance is in the form of the sky with zodiac signs around it.

The courtyard of the Philharmonic also has interesting architecture, including beautiful balconies, bay windows and fanciful rich moldings.

Odesa Academic Theater of Musical Comedy

This theater building was built in 1976–1981 in a style not typical for Odesa

Architect Henrich Topuz, to whom we owe the appearance of the Theater building, wanted to move away from the splendor and architectural excesses of socialist realism, so he turned to monumentalism. This approach resulted in a breakthrough in Soviet architecture. Besides the distinctive cube-shape form, the interior lobby, which can be viewed from outside, is mesmerizing.

Since 2012, the theater has been the main venue of *the Odesa International Film Festival* and holds the proud title of *the Festival Palace*

Clockwise: The building of the Odesa Academic Theater of Musical Comedy, 1980s
Fragment of the auditorium of the Odesa Academic Theater of Musical Comedy, 1980s
*Left page: Mykhailo Vodianoi as Papandopulo in the **Wedding in Malinovka** (Lenfilm, 1967)*

However, the purpose of the building's design was not limited to a unique appearance. One of the main aims was to ensure that the massive, heavy structure would not cause ruin to the dilapidated neighboring buildings. To do this, the engineers decided to not hammer columns, but insert them into pre-drilled holes filled with cement. This technique made the theater building, located on Pantelei-monivs'ka Street, one of the best and most thought-out projects of the Brezhnev era.

The theater is named after Mykhailo Vodianoi, who in 1976 became the first actor from the Operetta to receive the title of People's Artist of the USSR. Vodianoi's most well-known role was Papandopulo in the film *Wedding in Malinovka*. However, Vodianoi had a brilliant theater career, and the new theater building was built thanks to him. In addition, it was his initiative to name one of Odesa's streets after the popular singer and actor Leonid Utyosov.

Prior to the construction of the theater in 1981, the musical comedy troupe performed in **the Youth Theater on Hretska Street**. However, the theater quickly became too small for their increasingly popular shows. This eventually led to the construction of **the new Musical Comedy Theater**

22

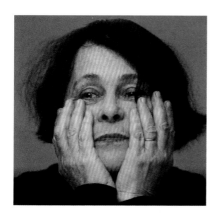

Kira Muratova

Muratova is a unique filmmaker, whose
work has always stood apart

Despite the fact that Kira Muratova was not born in Odesa,
all her work was connected
to this city. After graduating
from the VGIK in Moscow, she
began working at the Odesa
Film Studio, where she shot
her first full-length film,
entitled *Our Honest Bread*, in
1961. Her next films evoked
controversial reactions by
the leadership of the Odesa
Film Studio. Those films were
restricted at box offices and
censored, and eventually
forbidden. Due to that, Kira
Muratova moved to Saint
Petersburg (then Leningrad),
where she met her second
husband, who co-wrote the
scripts for her films. Eventually, she returned to Odesa.

Her film *The Asthenic
Syndrome* was filmed in Odesa
and received the Jury Grand
Prix at the Berlinale in 1990.

Kira Muratova
has lived in
Odesa since
1966. Although
her films clearly
show *the
influence of
the city*, she
speaks of it
rather harshly,
saying, "I'm not
from Odesa. I
came here by
chance and
stayed"

Clockwise: Still frame from Kira Muratova's **Brief Encounters** *(Odesa Film Studio, 1967);*
Still frame from **Three Stories** *(NTV Profit, 1997)*

In 2004, her film *The Tuner* was screened at the Venice Film Festival. The main character was played by the leader of the Odesa comic troupe the Masks. In 2010, at the first Odesa International Film Festival, a full retrospective of Kira Muratova's films was shown. In 2012, her most recent film *Eternal Redemption: The Casting* was shown at the Rome film festival. This film was the last of her career. It did not receive any awards, but was noted as a "hypnotic vortex" due to its original narrative structure. According to Muratova, she possesses a certain superiority complex, which is necessary in the film industry, but at the same time gives her a feeling of marginalized figure.

Muratova died on June 6, 2018, in Odesa.

The Tuner was the first and only film of Muratova's in which her characters kiss. She commented, "I've never seen a kiss in a movie that I liked. So I decided, why don't I give it a try!"

The Masks

The Masks are, without a doubt, Odesa's
most famous theater troupe

Heorhiy Deliev founded the Masks
theater in 1984 and has been its
artistic director for over 20 years.
The actors use pantomime and
clown techniques and have created
a unique style that differs from all
other comedy troupes. They were
founded upon the tradition of the
commedia dell'arte, the classics of
silent cinema, and the Theater of
the Absurd. Each time the troupe
performs it seems as though they
"live a small life" on stage with
their drama, pantomime and chore-
ography. Their unique performances
have been created and perfected
over many years.

In 1991, they created a new
platform for expression, the comical
silent TV program *The Masks Show*.
The series quickly became popular
in Ukraine and abroad. To date,
there have been about seventy skits
performed in the series, one full
film and twenty comedy episodes.
Many of the episodes have received
domestic and international awards.

In 2003, the comedy troupe
acquired its own theater called The
House of Clowns. For the opening of
the theater on Olhievska Street, the
premiere of Borys Barskyi's poetic
comedy *Othello* directed by Heorhiy
Deliev, was shown. The theater's

In 2017 the creators of "The Masks Show" announced that they will release *new series of the show*, which will be available in VR, and in a 360-degree review format

The troupe`s shows are bright and colorful, full of humour, gags, tricks and special effects

The Masks with one of their best casts: **Heorhiy Deliev, Borys Barskyi, Natalya Buzko** *and others*

repertoire also consists of well-known classics like *Romeo and Juliet*, *Don Juan*, *Orpheus and Eurydice*, and *Mozart and Salieri*. The theater also shows its own productions, such as Attack of the Clowns, The Odesa Orphan and many others.

24

Museum of Western and Eastern Art

Odesa's Museum of Western and Eastern Art is located in a former merchant's palace at the beginning of Pushkinska Street

This building was designed by architect Ludwig Otton in the style of eclecticism. The combination of Empire, Rococo, and elements of Baroque make it a great representative of Odesa's architecture. The interior of the building features intricate molding and carvings. The museum's permanent exhibition was put together from private collections and collections from Odesa University. Later it was enriched with artifacts from museums in Moscow and Kyiv.

Besides paintings, there are many sculptures, objects made from marble, and pieces of furniture. In the Eastern section you can find artifacts from Japan, China, Tibet and India.

The main showpieces of the permanent collection are the paintings

The stairway of the museum's grand entrance was made with famous **Carrara marble**, which is considered one of the most valuable types of stone. Famous objects made from Carrara marble include Michaelangelo's David, the Pantheon in Rome, and the Marble Arch in London. The stairway is also notable as it was made without supportive beams, making it look as though it is suspended in the air

The museum building is an architectural monument of national importance. It was designed in the middle of the 19th century by French architect L. Otton in the spirit of eclectics. To this day it is one of the most recognizable buildings in Odesa

*Top: Paul Alexandre Alfred Leroy, **Model**, 1893*
*Left page: Frans Hals, **St. Luke**, 1625*

St. Luke and *St. Matthew* by the Dutch portraitist Frans Hals from his cycle of the four evangelists. The portraits of *St. Mark* and *St. John* are stored in museums in Moscow and Los Angeles respectively. Another jewel of the exhibit is the painting *The Taking of Christ by Caravaggio*. In the summer of 2008, it was cut out of its frame and stolen from the museum. A year later the painting was found in Berlin and sent off for restoration. After the painting had been returned and an appraisal had been conducted, doubts were cast on whether it was actually the original or not.

25

Sviatoslav Richter

The early musical skills of this self-taught
and the most powerful virtuoso pianists
of the 20th century were acquired in Odesa

Sviatoslav Richter was born in Zhytomyr in 1915. In Odesa his father worked
as a teacher at the conservatory and as a church organist. He also played
the organ at the Odesa Opera House. Richter's father had a great influence
on him and ensured that he was not forced into the strict boundaries of
academic music. Instead of standard piano exercises, Richter immediately
began performing the music of Chopin and Wagner.

At the age of 15, Richter was offered a pianist position in the Vorontsov
Palace, and later in the Odesa Philharmonic. It was there that he held his
first solo concert, in which he played the works of Chopin. Soon after, Richter became an accompanist at the Odesa Opera House. Until 1941, Sviatoslav Richter was firmly grounded in Odesa. In 1937, he entered the Moscow
Conservatory but was almost immediately expelled. He returned briefly to
his native city, but quickly was back to his studies. His connection to Odesa
was interrupted by World War II. Richter became world-famous in the post-
war years. In 1960, he received the prestigious Grammy Award.

Richter also had a moment of fame on the big screen, when, in 1952, he starred in the film *The Composer Glinka (Kompozitor Glinka)*, by Soviet director Grigori Alexandrov. In the film Richter plays Hungarian composer and virtuoso pianist Franz Liszt. The film won awards at film festivals in both Locarno and in Mexico City

Richter played the piano at *Stalin's funeral*. After news of the dictator's death, he was hurriedly brought by military plane to Moscow from Tbilisi. The musician was apolitical. He did not know who Karl Marx was and actually did not care about the fact that Stalin was a former dictator. He himself recalled that moment well, saying, "I was playing the piano and saw up close the body of Stalin, along with Malenkov, and all the leaders. I played my music and left"

26

MoOMA and Artery

The Museum of Odesa Modern Art and the Artery gallery compliment each other, and are known as the heart of Odesa's art scene

The Museum of Modern Art in Odesa is a two-story building on Leontovycha Street. In addition to housing Odesa's modern art and being an architectural monument, it is a place of constant rebirth. For example, the Artery's "space for creative initiatives" regularly hosts exhibitions of the most exciting young artists of Odesa. Many of the visitors are from other cities or other countries. In addition to the museum and the art gallery, there is another pavilion, which hosts its own exhibits as well.

The MoOMA was founded on April 10, 2008, and has since been housed in several different locations. Finally, a truly ideal location was found that could accommodate both an impressive permanent exhibit and display new ambitious

Top: **The Fence Show**, *Odesa, 1967*
Left page: Oleksandr Roitburd, **Bird**, *1994*

One of the halls of the museum is dedicated to the famous forbidden *Fence Show* which was displayed in the summer of 1967 by Valentyn Khrushch and Stanislav Sychov. *The artists' works* were not accepted to the exhibition at the time and so they hung them on the temporary fence that enclosed the Opera theater during renovations. That's how should be Sychov and Khrushch went down in Odesa's history In the best traditions of postmodernism, before becoming *a museum of modern art,* the current building housed at different times: a counter-intelligence office of the Soviet Navy, the World Future Council, commercial offices and the Odesa Writers' Union

projects. The permanent exhibit consists of the most outstanding works of Odesan artists of the 20-21th centuries. A few spaces are devoted to a unique phenomenon of Odesa art, the so-called "group of nonconformists" and Odesa concep-tualism. There has been a diverse and impressive collection of inde-pendent projects, geared toward various platforms such as the Odesa Biennale or numerous other special-ized international projects.

27

Odesa Conceptualism

Odesa conceptualism is an art phenomenon native to the city. It has been recognized far beyond the borders of both Odesa and Ukraine

Conceptualism in an Odesa context was not just a play of images or levels of meanings, nor the confrontation of reality and absurdity. To a much greater degree it was centered around a synergy of young and ingenious artists, for whom the idea behind a project was often more important than its implementation. The Odesa school of Conceptualism is said to have originated in 1982 when Leonid Voitsekhov and Serhiy Anufriyev met. Later, friends and acquaintances who were similar in spirit joined their group, which is why in the beginning Odesa conceptualism existed in the format of an endless party. Ideas for exhibitions, installations and performances arose spontaneously while walking around the flea market, walking between artists' workshops, or partaking in other activities, since the group was always together. Leonid Voitsekhov is considered the founding father and leader of the Odesa school of Conceptualism, thanks to

One of the most famous performances of that time was *The Method of Killing with a Flag,* written in 1984 by Yuri Leiderman and Ihor Chatskin. As the name implies, the artists had the idea to rethink the purpose of the sacred state symbol, using it as a weapon

Clockwise: Performance **Exploration of Artistic Deposits,** *1987*
Performance **Ways of Killing Someone with a Flag,** *1984*
Left page: Leonid Voitsekhov, **Direct Speech,** *1984*

Ihor Stepin and Svitlana Martynchyk who created the group Martynchyky, were an integral part of the Odesa school of conceptualism and the creators of the writer Max Frye. The first texts published under this pseudonym were written in co-authorship. Later books were written by Svitlana alone

his charisma, his particular knowledge, and his knack for being able to infinitely generate new ideas.

The next step in the development of Odesa conceptualism was the interaction between Odesan and Muscovite artists. It remained very important that the Odesa school did not blend too closely with that of Moscow. The works of the Odesan artists differed in their more elegant humor and lesser focus on social art. Despite overlap which united the individual artists in a "club," each of them used his or her own tools. It might have been a sealed text which could not be understood without knowing the context behind it, or a deliberate contrast to a style of street ads with absurd inscriptions. Unfortunately, most of the Odesa conceptualists eventually moved on to Moscow, and later became dispersed throughout the world. Due to this, the school ceased to exist. However, at the beginning of the 20th century there was a renewed interest in the history of its ideas and directions, which resulted in numerous exhibitions in both Odesa and Kyiv. You can see examples of the Odesa school of conceptualism at the Odesa Museum of Modern Art on no. 5 Leontovycha Street.

28

Odesa Museum of Art

The museum has over ten thousand works on display

The Odesa Museum of Art is located at the very center of the city, in Naryshkin Palace. In 1888 the palace was bought by prominent public figure and collector Gregory Marazli, who gave it to the city. It took 9 more years to complete the first collection. Finally, the opening of the museum took place on the November 6, 1899.

The museum's display covers 26 floors and follows a chronological order, starting with works dating from the 16th and 17th centuries and finishing with 21st century pieces. The museum owns an extensive collection of Orthodox icons from the 16th to the 19th centuries, that gives a complete picture of the icons' features and includes artistic works of a high level. Its collection counts, among many fine pieces, one of Ukraine's largest collections of Ivan Aivazovsky, with 28 pictures, and also pieces by Arkhyp Kuindzhi, Ilya Repin, Mikhail Vrubel, and Wassily Kandinsky.

At the modern art department you can find a number of works created after 1920, including pieces from the Odesan nonconformist movement.

Every type of visual art can be found in the museum collection: *fine art, graphic art and sculpture*

Since 2017 the museum has been headed by the Ukrainian artist *Oleksandr Roitburd*

Clockwise: Zinaida Serebriakova, **Harvest**, *1915; Oleksandr Atsmanchuk,* **Flight**, *1965; Pavlo Sorokin,* **Hercules and Lichas**, *1849*

29

Vinyl Market

Vinyl record lovers will surely enjoy a trip to Odesa's vinyl market at Shevchenko Park

Shevchenko Park is a wonderful place for many reasons. Located within its parameters are the Zelenyi Teatr (Green Theater), the Walk of Fame, and the Quarantine Wall, and it has a great view of the sea and port. The park also hosts a worthwhile attraction for record enthusiasts: a weekly vinyl record market, located near the fountain to the left of the Taras Shevchenko monument. Every Sunday, from 11am until 2pm, you can combine a walk in the park with a record shopping trip. In addition to admiring both vintage and new vinyl records, the sellers themselves are quite intriguing. If you strike up a

Despite the apparent harmless hobby of collecting records, in Soviet times, such gatherings suffered ruthless crackdowns. Vinyl lovers had to continually find new meeting spots until they eventually began to gather in the park at their current spot near the fountain period In the unlikely event that you don't find the record you are looking for, you can try **the Starokinnyi flea market** There, in addition to records, you can find practically any other object you may possibly need!

conversation with any of them, the time will surely fly by quickly. These veteran record merchants all have their own opinions and can debate tirelessly on various topics, including music and sport, politics and really anything else.

Vinyl lovers have been gathering here for over 40 years, beginning in the seventies. At that time, these meetings were the only opportunity to hear a new Beatles or Pink Floyd album. Even today one can find both the most recent records as well as real rarities.

30

Odesa International Film Festival

Odesa is considered to be a city of cinema. Since 2010, it has held one of the largest International Film Festivals in Eastern Europe

The festival mainly focuses on feature-length mainstream art films. Since 2012, it has held both an international and a Ukraine-wide competition. Unlike most festivals, the Grand Prix is awarded on the basis of audience voting. The main festival prize is the Golden Duke, an updated version of the award from the eponymous Odesa festival in 1988. Apart from the main award, the jury awards prizes for best film, best director and best actor/actress. In the few years the festival has been running, jury chairman have included Jos Stelling, Peter Webber, and Jerzy Stuhr.

Every summer, the festival hosts a Summer Film School, where world-class filmmakers share their knowledge while teaching master classes.

In addition to the open shows on the Potemkin Steps, there are film screenings on Lanzheronivskyi Uzviz. In 2011, the Argentine film **Antenna** was shown there, accompanied by the music of the Franco-Ukrainian band Esthetic Education. This was the last performance of the group, which broke up shortly afterward

In 2015, one of the festival's VIP guests was *Darren Aronofsky*, director of the films *Requiem for a Dream, The Fountain, and Pi*. In addition to teaching a master class, Darren participated in the international event #shellno. The event was a protest against Shell's drilling in the Arctic. While kayaking near Odesa beach, Aronofsky and his friends held up a giant poster with the slogan #shellno

The festival also holds tribute film screenings the directors who have contributed to the history of cinema.

The most widely attended events in the festival are the open-air film screenings on the Potemkin Steps. One of the most popular show was held in 2015 — it was *Man with a Movie Camera* screened to the musical accompaniment of Michael Nyman's neoclassical minimalist orchestra.

31

Mute Nights Festival

Every summer in Odesa, silent films accompanied by live music are shown along the Black Sea in the evening

The Mute Nights Festival was established in 2010. From the very first show, the purpose was to popularize silent archival films and film classics. Most of the films showed are those from the 1920s and 1930s produced by Ukrainian or foreign directors. A variety of musicians are attracted by the opportunity to create entirely new musical concepts.

It is worth noting that all this happens on late summer evenings, or rather nights, right on the beach. The usual location for the festival is the yacht-club berth at the Odesa Sea Port.

It is not surprising that this festival takes place in

The Silent Nights festival was quite closely connected with the Odesa JazzFest through its director **Yuri Kuznetsov**. He participated as a musician in almost all of the Silent Nights events

*Left page: Still frame from **A Trip to the Moon** (Star Film, 1902)*

Odesa, as it was here that the first Ukrainian film studio appeared, and also where world silent film masterpieces such as *Man with a Movie Camera*, *Battleship Potemkin*, and *Zvenihora* were shot.

Not much compares to an evening of silent film near the quiet Black Sea, listening to the cries of gulls and the soft rustling of the surf. This is one of the most unusual festivals in Odesa, which is definitely worth a visit. It is almost impossible to see these films anywhere else.

The festival has **no exact dates**. It has taken place in June, July and August. Therefore, those wishing to attend will have to check for upcoming announcements

32

Odesa Photo Days

The festival calls itself a non-profit platform for photographers and anyone interested in photography

The festival first took place in 2015 and was held in two cities: in April in Odesa, and in September in Batumi, Georgia. Originally the two cities had the same festival program, but in 2017 the organizer divided the festival into two separate branches, citing Georgia's and Ukraine's different cultural and historical contexts.

The festival's events are held on several different sites; in addition to photography exhibits, there is also an educational program: lectures, masterclasses and presentations all run throughout the festival.

Kateryna Radchenko, the festival's main organizer, states that it was created as a response to topical events, meaning that each year a new theme is chosen that reflects current events happening in society.

Odesa Photo Days festival has become well-known in different parts of the world, appeared on the international map of photo events and has implemented a number of special projects, both in Ukraine and abroad.

This is *Ukraine's first photography festival,* which attracts photographers, curators, and people from the art world every year

A photo-competition for teenagers, called *Future Days* is also held at the festival, which aims to show how younger people see the world

FOOD

33

Forshmak

You haven't really been to Odesa if you
did not try its trademark dish, forshmak

This popular local dish was invented back in the 15th century in Prussia and Sweden. However, the current common
preparation was adopted from 18th century Jewish culinary
tradition. Since then, it has become an integral part of Odesa
cuisine in almost every home. The recipe is extremely simple
and, at the same time, obscure. In its classic form, it is a cold
appetizer of herring, mashed together with apple, boiled egg,
onion and butter. It is perfect on a hot summer afternoon,
spread on black bread and sprinkled with chopped herbs.

Besides forshmak,
gefilte fish,
or stuffed fish,
is another Jewish
culinary dish that is
popular in Odesa.
It is traditionally
served during
holidays. In Isaac
Babel's *Odessa*
Tales, the dish is
featured on the
wedding table
along with fish
soup

Even though this is a Jewish, and not Ukrainian dish, it is impossible to come up with something that is more quintessentially characteristic of Odesa cuisine.

Forshmak remains popular in Odesa restaurants and in family homes. Most families have their own special forshmak recipes, which can include cottage cheese, cabbage, or potatoes. Some even prepare it with lamb or pork.

The slang term "forshmak" is used at the Odesa prison to refer to the very *lowest caste prisoners*. The slang verb *"forshmachyty" (to "forshmak")* means to confuse someone

34

Eggplant Caviar

This classic Odesa appetizer with Greek and Jewish roots is referred to as "blue caviar" by the locals

As with forshmak and sprat fish cakes, there are dozens of options in Odesa for making eggplant caviar. Besides caviar, eggplant is prepared in many other ways, such as stewing it in cream sauce, cooking it with onions, or even preparing it with jam.

The basis of the eggplant caviar recipe is a blackened baked eggplant, from which the rind is removed. It is then finely chopped with a knife and mixed with tomatoes, garlic, onions, herbs, black pepper, and sunflower oil in a deep bowl and left to cool. It is often served as a snack or spread on bread with salted cheese. Some recipes call for baked bell peppers, and others use olive oil instead of sunflower.

In his memoirs, the famous Odesan writer Valentyn Katayev wrote that baked eggplant should only be cut with a wooden knife. This is because the blue color of the eggplant is lost when it comes into contact with metal. Therefore, according to some, this is the only way to make the authentic recipe.

Eggplant caviar was very common in the USSR, and its popularity was played out in the famous Soviet comedy *Ivan Vasilievich.* After joking about *overseas caviar being made out of eggplants*, it became a popular dish

35

Fish cakes

Not many people know about Odesa's gastronomic traditions. However, you don't have to look far to sample some of the trademarks of the local cuisine

Odesa's traditional dishes reflect the diversity of a multiethnic port city. Needless to say, the importance of fish and seafood cannot be overestimated. Flounder, herring, gobies, mussels and mollusk are all an integral part of the diet of Odesa residents. A special place is occupied by Black Sea sprat, which can be bought fresh or salted in barrels. The most common dish with sprat is fish cakes. To prepare it, clean the fish,

Fish cakes taste best when made with freshly caught fish. In Odesa, you can buy fresh fish *at the fishing port at 5 or 6 am.* Purchasing the morning's catch from fishermen is usually much cheaper than buying them at Odesa markets during the day

then mix it with eggs, salt, flour and pepper. Form it into patties or cakes and fry them on both sides in hot oil.

A typical Odesa breakfast consists of sprat fish cakes with black rye bread and lemon juice. The fish cakes can be served in a variety of ways. Some like them with onions and pickles, others, with herbs or special sauces.

36

Pryvoz Market

This is a place where you can chat with the intelligentsia, hear the latest news, or try exquisite appetizers

Odesa's main market can be a very interesting, if unusual, site for tourism. The Pryvoz Market was established shortly after the founding of Odesa. Initially, it was an appendage of the Old Market, which didn't to survive. The name Pryzov, which roughly means *imported goods*, derives from the fact that goods were sold directly from carts after they had arrived in the seaport. In its early days, the market was a dirty and disorganized unpaved square. Gradually, it expanded and was built up.

There is a monument to *"Aunt Sonia"* on the territory of the market, which was installed in 2007. The sculpture is dedicated to Madame Storozhenko, the heroine of Valentin Katayev's novel *Lone White Sail*

Due to the dirt and unsanitary conditions at the Pryvoz Market, it was inhabited by a very large number of rats. They were ultimately the cause of a fire, which burned down the whole market period. In 1902, when the plague broke out in Odesa yet again, Pryvoz was one of the main points of infection. Odesans decided to burn the dirtiest stalls, but the flames destroyed the entire market. After the fire, the market was rebuilt, including the fruit section, which had been the main architectural landmark before the fire.

Pryvoz was the birthplace of the famous "Odesa language," a mixture of Jewish, Russian, Ukrainian, and Moldovan words with a characteristic pronunciation. It became a defining feature of Odesans.

Next to the "Aunt Sonia" there is *a statue of an Odesa cat* rubbing against the foot of Aunt Sonia in anticipation of fish

37

Odesa Sparkling

The oldest winery in Ukraine is located
on one of Odesa's most beautiful streets

At the end of the 20th century, wealthy French entrepreneur Henri Roederer had the idea of producing sparkling wine in Odesa. He bought a former noble villa on Frantsuzskyi Boulevard to convert into a factory. At the same time, Russian Emperor Nicholas II issued a decree establishing the South-Russian Winemaking Society of Henri Roederer. From that moment on began the history of winemaking in Odesa.

A year and a half later, the construction of the factory was completed and the production of sparkling wine began. Roederer's goal was to create a sparkling wine at the quality of original French Champagne. To do so, he purchased some French equipment and invited French specialists to work in his winery. Even the architect was French. He designed a four-story building, two stories of which were

There is another winery of the same name on Frantsuzkyi Boulevard. It is notable that this wintery *used catacombs under Odesa as its wine cellars*. The network of old wine cellars is located around the winery. According to rumors, some cellars have secret exits into homes, as well as on the slopes of the sea. It is also rumored that huge wooden barrels of brandy spirits and wine are still there from those times

located underground. The entry arch has become a symbol of the winery.

Hard work and attention to detail made it possible to produce the best dry and sparkling wines in the whole south of Ukraine. A few years after its opening, the plant received its first award, a medal from the 1904 World Exhibition. But the winery's further growth was prevented by the Russian Revolution and two world wars. Up until 1952, the winery produced no wine and was used at first to produce macaroni, then as a warehouse, and later as an aviation repair shop. After 1952, the winery renewed its original purpose and began to produce wine.

38

ФАЛАФЕЛЬ

Falafel

Odesa's main street food is, of course, falafel. It is on the menu of most local restaurants, but there is only one real falafel "maestro"

At the intersection of Preobrazhen-ska and Troitska Streets there is a street vendor called Maestro Falafel. This legendary place has become a must-visit for tourists and a favorite place for anyone who's tried their food before. Once you find the place, you might have to wait in a long line made up of office clerks, artists, builders and photographers, most of whom work within a 10-block radius.

This traditional Arabic sandwich is made of ground cooked chickpeas which are formed into balls and deep fried. Traditional hummus is made from blended chickpeas, olive oil, garlic, lemon juice, pa-

First opened in 1996, *Maestro Falafel* was dismantled in 2016. Thankfully, it was later reopened, and the falafel is supposed to be even better than before

prika, and a sesame paste. This is wrapped in lavash bread with fresh vegetables and aromatic spices. Many people go to Odesa in search of this particular falafel, finding it pointless to try falafel elsewhere. This fast-food joint is a favorite of vegetarians, since chickpeas contains a lot of protein, and are rich in various vitamins, amino acids and trace elements. Many people also purchase ready-made fried chickpea balls to add to a homemade falafel, since preparing them can be difficult and time consuming. Most admit, though, that preparing a falafel at home which tastes as good as at Maestro is impossible.

39

Dizyngoff

A restaurant by day, and a bar by night —
Dizyngoff stands out among other venues
in Odesa

Dizyngoff is difficult to call a restaurant or a bar; rather, it's a creative space for everyone who wants to get experience in gastronomy, music and art. The name of the institution was not chosen by chance. Its main message is in the image of a charismatic person, the first mayor of Tel Aviv — Meir Dizengoff. Being a great innovator, he created the city of Tel Aviv from scratch in the desert. Odesa's Dizyngoff, according to its owners, is also about city innovation. Moreover, the symbol of the venue is a dove with a human face, symbolizing a socially active citizen.

The cuisine in Dizyngoff is a mix of Japanese, Peruvian and French, with oriental accents, but not kosher. The menu is regularly updated since its chef, Nika Lozovskaya, is in an endless creative search for new recipes. She is not afraid to mix different culinary trends and styles; she doesn't play by the rules in her kitchen.

In the morning, Dizyngoff works as a restaurant; in the evening as a bar. It's a meeting point for the creative, intellectual circles of Odesa. Dizyngoff stands alone among other venues of the city.

40

Brothers Grill

Almost all dishes in the restaurant are cooked on an open fire

The restaurant "Brothers Grill" or Bratya Grill is located on Derybasivska Street. It was the first restaurant in Ukraine that invited top chefs and bartenders to make guest appearances from other areas of Ukraine or from other countries. These culinary stars have taken on developing special menus, training chefs and delighting guests with their own cooking. Guests' top favorites are then added to the main menu.

The philosophy of the "Grill Brothers" restaurant is the principle of soul food, that is, "We feed from the heart," as if in a home or family atmosphere. The central spot in the restaurant's open kitchen is occupied by the only Argentinean grill in Odesa, which is 2.5 meters long. The menu has juicy steaks, meat and fish dishes, favorite Odesa delicacies, as well as a variety of salads and side dishes.

The unique interior, created by the studio of Denys Belenko, underscores the very unique soulful atmosphere of "Grill Brothers," taking into account the best traditions of ancient Odesa. Belenko updates the interior regularly, adding new and interesting details and accents. One of these is the snow-white chandelier, made of

Mykhailo Serebrin, the restaurant's co-owner, recommends the turkey baked with pear and apple sauce, the burger, and the ribeye steak

9,000 champagne corks. A friendly cockatoo parrot named Rio, who loves getting acquainted with patrons, lives in the restaurant.

The restaurant's atmosphere is made complete with a musical selection that matches the restaurant itself, including golden classics of jazz, turntable hits, and the melodies of virtuoso pianists.

PLACES

41

The Potemkin Steps

This masterpiece of classicist architecture was designed by Francesco Boffo in 1841 and has become one of the city's best-known features

These stairs were first constructed in order to connect the port with the city of Odesa. Before Odesa was established and the Turkish fortress of Eni-Dunya existed in its place, steps had been carved into the soft limestone.

Initially, the Potemkin Steps consisted of 200 steps and went right down to the water. However, due to the expansion of the port's boardwalk there are now only 192 steps and 10 landings. The proportions of the staircase were designed so that when you look down, the stairs don't look narrower at the bottom. This effect was achieved due to the gradual increase in the

In 1902 there was a funicular next to the stairs, which operated in both directions. In the 1970s, it was replaced by *an escalator*, which

functioned until the mid 1990s. In 2005, in honor of the 211th anniversary of the founding of the city, the funicular was reopened

Each year there is *a running race up and down* the Potemkin Steps. Anyone can participate. To date, the record is 22.8 seconds

width of the landings going downward. Thus, the parapets seem to be parallel to each other and make the construction appear monumental. The size and grandeur of this staircase is matched only by the Spanish Steps in Rome.

The current name for the stairs was coined after the famous scenes from Sergei Eisenstein's *Battleship Potemkin* were filmed here. At different times they were called the Bulvarni Steps, the Richelieu Steps, or the Gigantic Steps. In 2015, the European academy of cinema recognized the Potemkin Steps as a "treasure of European film culture."

42

Opera Theater

Odesa's Opera Theater is considered one of the city's main attractions

The city's first opera theater was opened in 1810, only 15 years after the founding of Odesa. It was designed by French architect Thomas de Thomon and made of wood.

The new structure, built in 1887, was designed by architects Fellner and Helmer. They had designed similar projects in Vienna, Budapest and Salzburg. The building is designed in the image of the Dresden Opera. However, since the authors were not able to come to Odesa, they could not fully work out the plans, which were carried out by local architects together with Alexander Bernardazzi.

The structure is designed in the style of Viennese baroque and the facade is richly decorated with sculptural groups. They represent comedy and tragedy and fragments from Greek plays, as well as the busts of famous composers; the interior of the theater is in the style of late rococo.

Clockwise: Pyotr Tchaikovsky; Isadora Dunkan; Nikolai Rimsky-Korsakov; Sergei Rachmaninov; Enrico Caruso; Feodor Chaliapin

Since the Opera House is on fairly weak soil, the base needs to be regularly reinforced. During one such restoration in the 1950s, more than 6 million litres of *liquid glass* was poured under the foundation. It were the first such procedure with this amount of sodium silicate undertaken in the USSR

In the center of the ceiling is a two-ton crystal chandelier, surrounded by four scenes from Shakespeare. Caruso, Chaliapin and Isadora Duncan have performed on Odesa's Opera stage and Tchaikovsky, Rimsky-Korsakov and Rachmaninov have all conducted in this theater.

43

City Garden

This was the city's first park, established just nine years after the city was founded

The land where the City Garden is located previously belonged to Felix de Ribas, the city founder's brother. In 1803, he began establishing his own small park with his own funds. But after a few years, he realized that it had become too expensive for him, and decided to donate his park to the city. Odesa did not have much green space at the time. Thus, the new city park quickly became one of the most popular places for Odesans to spend free time. Seedlings were specially ordered from Spain and Italy; a bronze sculpture composition of a lion and a lioness "guarding" the main entrance was brought from France.

The park also has a monument to Kisya and Osya the characters of Ilf and Petrov's novel, *Golden Calf*, and a monument to the great Odesa singer.

Additionally, a sculpture of the famous chair from the book *Twelve Chairs* was installed there, and the five-square-meter radius around the chair was recognized as Odesa's smallest square.

For many years, the park has been a gathering place for artists to exhibit their work in the open space. But in recent years, they have moved to Soborna Square, the favorite spot of chess players.

Adjacent to Soborna Square and the City Garden is *Sadova Street*. The name comes from the word for gardeners and was named after the gardeners who initially worked there in the times of Jose and Felix de Ribas

The former house of Felix de Ribas now houses the restaurant *Klarabara* on the ground floor

44

The Passage

Odesa's Passage has more sculptural and stucco decorations than any other location in Odesa, even the renowned Opera Theater

Odesa's main street Derybasivska ends spectacularly with the Passage building. Grandiose and richly decorated with stucco, the building is unique to Odesa architecture. The covered shopping arcade with its transparent roof is combined with an adjacent hotel complex. The Passage was built in just two years, 1898-1899, and its creator was the architect and engineer Lev Vlodek. Initially, the building was supposed to be built near the Novyi Bazaar, but in the end the owner turned down this idea. The Passage was built on Derybasivska, and a circus was built on the spot by the bazaar.

After the construction was completed, the Passage became one of the greatest buildings in Odesa, and even had one of the first prototypes of an elevator. It was specially shown to Russian Emperor Nicholas I. At the time, the building housed

The Passage Hotel and shopping area are considered one of the heights of creativity of the architect *Lev Vlodek*, along with the House with the Atlantes on Hohol Street and the Grand Moscow Hotel on no. 29 Derybasivska Street

the most elite and prestigious shops; one of them was the Odesa branch of the Fabergé jeweler.

Just one year after its opening, the first fire occurred in the Passage building, damaging the roof and other areas. The damage was quickly repaired, apart from the destroyed turret on the corner, which has not yet been reconstructed. Today, you can see the sculptures Fortuna and Mercury on the roof on the side near the City Garden. Mercury, the patron of trade, is sitting on a steam train, while the goddess of fortune is looking at the sea in the distance, illuminating a path with her torch.

45

Tolstoy Palace

Despite its advanced age and rocky history, this building has been preserved almost in its original form

The two-story palace on Tolstoy Street, which has twelve rooms, was built in 1832. In 1897, an adjacent art gallery was built. Now the Tolstoy Palace functions as the House of Scientists, which runs a number of scientific conferences.

The building was constructed in the style of Russian Classicism. This architectural ensemble is characterized by eclecticism and a variety of decorative elements. As befits a real palace, the house is full of secrets. For example, one of the mirrors is actually a door to a secret room. Moreover, one of the lounges, where concerts and speeches are given, has excellent acoustics. If you stand in one particular spot, everything you say will be clearly heard throughout the whole room, but if you move a little bit from the spot, you

This is one of Odesa's most beautiful buildings, designed by legendary *Boffo* — the author of the Potemkin Stairs

*Left page: Domenico Morelli, portrait of the young **Elena Smirnova**, who later became the wife of Count Tolstoy. She was a peasant, but that didn't stop young Tolstoy from marrying her and having a family with her. Some say her ghost still lives in the house*

will only be heard by the person standing next to you. Each room is beautiful in its own way, especially after the palace's restoration.

The history of the dynasty who lived here is no less interesting than the history of the building itself. The Tolstoy family donated Odesa its first telephone and an ambulance, the first one in the Russian Empire. According to legend, the telephone was created to ensure that the count could listen to opera in his office. The Tolstoy family also established the Institute for Noble Maidens, and a charitable society for helping the poor. They also sponsored the construction of the Opera House and Public Library (now the Gorky Library).

There is a piano in one of the rooms which some claim *Franz Liszt* played on

46

Vorontsov Lighthouse

In 1927 the lighthouse was renovated by Odesa Governor-General Mykhailo Vorontsov and named in his honour

With the expansion of the port, the need appeared for a new lighthouse. In 1845, a wooden lighthouse was built on Karantynnyi upon the initiative of Arctic explorer Mikhail Lazarev.

Twenty years later, a cast-iron 17-meter lighthouse was built in its place. It served until 1941, when it was blown up during the siege of the city. A new lighthouse was built in 1954 and traditionally named after Vorontsov. Its white walls and red lights are the first thing ships see upon approaching Odesa's harbor. The lighthouse has become a symbol of Odesa along with the Potemkin Steps, the Opera House and the monument to Richelieu.

The legendary lighthouse caretaker *Ivan Tsykhovych* has been working in the lighthouse since 1956. He has dedicated 60 years of his life to one of Odesa's most well known symbols

Left page: Ivan Tsykhovych

The Stvornyi lighthouse is located at the pinnacle of building **no.5 on Preobrazhenska Street**. It works in tandem with the Vorontsov lighthouse to help ships that call at the port. If the ship is on the right course, it is possible to simultaneously observe both lighthouses since they are located above one another visually. Due to the difference in heights, ships can determine exactly which way to make corrections in direction. The height of the lighthouse above sea level is 54.9 meters

Tours are regularly offered to the lighthouse from the Odesa port, along a 600-meter causeway and jetty. On each side of the jetty, bollards from old Turkish cannons have been embedded in the concrete. They were taken during the Crimean War as trophies. The lighthouse is situated in the most narrow point of the bay, which allows for the observation of incoming ships as closely as possible. On its wall is a bell that can be used as a signal, should there be complete failure of the security systems.

There is *a regular lightkeeper* in the port, though today the beacon is managed remotely

47

The Odesa Caverns

One of the world's biggest underground labyrinths

No one knows for certain exactly when the first underground tunnels appeared in Odesa; however, it is likely that the caves expanded greatly when the city was first being developed in the 18th century.

Quarries make up the larger part of the caverns. The stone extracted from these quarries was used to build the new city of Odesa; limestone was quarried there right up until the beginning of the 20th century.

After the Bolshevik Revolution, the tunnels were taken over by criminals and were used for smuggling. During the Nazi occupation of Odesa, the tunnels were used by the partisan resistance as a hideout. Today, if you go to the Museum of the Glory of the Partisans in the nearby village of Nerubaiske, you can see one of the sections of the caves that has been preserved exactly as it was when it was used by the partisans during the war.

Tours to other sections of the caves are not officially allowed because the tunnels are unsafe. Still, there are a lot of people who explore the caves despite the dangers involved.

The Odesa caverns stretch to *about two and a half thousand metres in length, with a depth of up to thirty metres*

Nearly half of the historical center of the city is built on top of the caverns, which, admittedly, is rather unsafe. For this reason Odesa does not have *an underground metro system*

Clockwise: Fidel Castro in the Odesa caverns, 1981; one of the tunnels in the Odesa caverns
Left page: Map of the Odesa caverns

48

The Colonnade

Odesa's colonnade offers the city's best platform for stunning views of the harbor and the Gulf of Odesa

Odesa's famous colonnade is located on the grounds of the Vorontsov Palace, built for former Odesa governor-general Mikhail Vorontsov. Previously, there was a greenhouse in its place, in which exotic fruits were grown.

Located on the edge of the hill, the palace was a great place from which to observe the growing port. The colonnade was designed by Francesco Boffo, who also designed the Potemkin Steps. It consists of ten pairs of columns covered with a gable roof. The supple contour of the Belvedere Colonnade makes it a great viewing platform. From it, you can watch a sunrise over the sea or a sunset over the slopes of Odesa. Its favorable location at the

Not far from the colonnade is *an ancient well full of Carrara marble*. Before its restoration, it served for many years as a card table for lovers of cards and dominoes

beginning of the Prymorskyi Boulevard near Teshchyn Bridge has made it a popular meeting spot for Odesans.

In addition to being a viewing platform, the colonnade has its own secrets. For example, that there was a walled door on the outer side of the base. According to urban legend, it used to be a restaurant or tavern. The owner lured patrons to it, mostly women, and got them drunk. Then he took his victims through the underground passage to the catacombs. From there they were transported into slavery to Turkish galleys or brothels. This story is a myth, and there are no signs of any door having been there.

Currently, the colonnade is used during various festivals or simply for sightseeing.

On Odesa's 200-year anniversary, sculptor Mykhailo Reva turned the well into *a fountain*. The fountain blends in well into the overall style of the palace

49

Courtyards

There are probably only two cities that are famous for their courtyards — St. Petersburg and Odesa

Odesa courtyards are a world of their own, with a unique language, laws, smell and charm. In the summer they usually smell like baked peppers and fried fish. They are a place where you can hear the latest gossip and news before anyone else.

A common way for people to socialize is to visit each other's houses. Sometimes the balconies surround the perimeter of the courtyard in an Italian style. Thus it is possible to get from apartment to apartment by walking along the balcony.

Often old cars, improvised flowerbeds made from tires, and signage from the last century can be found in Odesa courtyards. And it is impossible to imagine an Odesa courtyard without laundry hanging on a clothesline. Together with Odesa's cats, they are a mandatory part of an Odesa-style courtyard.

There are courtyards in Odesa to suit every taste. There are courtyards similar to those in St. Petersburg. There are tiny, cozy courtyards. There are grand ones with centuries-old trees and marble wells. In one of the courtyards on Pasteur Street, you can go through several courtyards and arrive at a parallel street.

Another courtyard on *no.37 Osypova Street* has a miniature replica of the Eiffel Tower. In the courtyard of building *no.3 on Torhova Street* is a beautiful statue of a dolphin. And in the courtyard on *no.46 Pasteur Street*, there is a monument to Kyriak Kostandi. It was in this building that the artist lived and worked. In the courtyard at *no.1-3 Matrosiv Provulok*, the "Black Night" oak, Odesa's oldest tree, is growing

The courtyard of Vorontsovskyi Lane is very well known. In it is an concealed ladder, through which you can get down to Voyennyi Uzviz. This allows you to greatly shorten your path, by not having to go over Teshchyn Bridge. In the courtyard of the building with the Atlantes on Hohol Street, you can enjoy excellent views of the sea, the port and the colonnade. In some courtyards you can find old monuments and rare old trees. At no.17 Torhova street, a "Pushkin" poplar is growing. The tree is more than 200 years old, making it the same age as the city.

In one of the courtyards at **no.15 Velykyi Fontan station** is the world's only monument of the Swedish book character Karlsson-on-the-roof. It was made by hand by one of the local residents

50

Building with Atlantes

While Odesa has an incredible number of buildings with atlantes and caryatids, the one on Hohol Street stands out

The atlantid on this building differs from many others of its kind. Rather than it being a bas-relief on a wall or column, as with other buildings, here it forms a composition of its own. In it, two atlantes are bent under the weight of the world, on top of which the spectacular se-cond-floor balcony sits. The building itself is a complex asymmetrical U-shaped structure. It is framed by a cozy yard, which is closed off with fencing and two symmetrical iron gates.

The house originally belonged to the aristocratic Falz-Fein family.

The Falz-Fein family had a close relationship with *Dostoevsky and Nabokov.* In his autobiography, *Other Shores,* **Nabokov** mentioned the first wife of his uncle *Dmitri Nabokov, Lydia Falz-Fein.* The dynasty maintained these relations in pre-revolutionary Russia and in exile

An image of the atlantes on this building is used as the emblem of *the World Club of Odesans*

Left page: Eduard von Falz-Fein, grandfather of Baron von Falz-Fein

This dynasty was famous for its patronage and collections of Russian paintings and icons. Their collections have been passed on to many museums in Russia and Ukraine.

When Odesa was occupied by German troops, one of the Nazi generals took over the building.

During his stay, the sculpture of the atlantes had a Nazi swastika drawn on it. Now of course, the symbol has been removed and the building has become a popular place for tourists and others who stroll along Hohol Street.

51

Laocoön Statue

According to Greek legend, Laocoön was a priest of the god Apollo

Together with his sons, Laocoön warned against allowing the famous Trojan horse into Troy. However, at the very moment that he was doing so, two snakes crawled out of the sea and strangled the priest and his sons. The Trojans took this as a good sign and allowed the gift to enter the Greek city. After that, Troy fell. This story served as the inspiration for the famous sculpture of Laocoön and his sons. The original statue was made by Greek sculptors from Rhodes in the 1st century BC. Later, it disappeared and was found again in Rome in 1506. Now the sculpture is kept in the Vatican and is considered a world-class attraction.

The world's only full-sized replica of this statue can be found in front of Odesa's Archaeological Museum. Initially, it was commissioned for Odesa mayor Hryhoriy Marazli's dacha. He saw the original while on a tour around Europe, and immediately ordered one for himself. In the 1920s the statue was located on Odesa's Trykutynyi (Triangular) Square. It was vandalized several times, after which it was transferred to its new place in front of the Archaeological Museum. It has become one of Odesa's main attractions.

The original sculpture was found when it was accidentally dug up in a vineyard in Rome in 1506. It was restored by *a pupil of Michelangelo* and installed in the Belvedere garden in a special niche

The Odesa replica is made of high-quality Carrara marble. This marble was also used to carve the stone staircase in *the Odesa Museum of Western and Oriental Art* and elements in the Odesa Philharmonic

Clockwise: Caricature of the Laocoön group as apes, 16th Century; Richard Wallace, Laocoön; William Blake, Laocoön; Giovanni Antonio da Brescia, Laocoön Group, 1506; Francesco Hayez, Laocoön, 1812; El Greco, Laocoön, 1610–1614

52

Lutheran Cathedral

The St. Paul Lutheran Cathedral is the religious center of all German Lutherans in Ukraine

In 1804, Count Richelieu appointed the first Lutheran pastor in Odesa. In 1812, Odesa became the residence of the Lutheran bishop. The foundation of the church was laid in 1824, but in June of that same year, the building collapsed. Due to this, it took three more years for the construction of the church to be completed. However, in 1838 there was a strong earthquake in Odesa, which damaged the building. At the end of the 19th century, the decision was made to rebuild the church, so that it could accommodate more than a thousand people.

At the time, the church spire made it the tallest building in Odesa, and from the turret, one could see the whole city. After the Russian revolution, the church was looted and closed down. After the war, it was turned into a gym. These transformations led not only to the destruction of the building, but also the desecration of the church as a religious monument. In 1976, the building burned down. Many people believe that it was caused by arson; however, the perpetrators were never found. After the fire, the building wasn't repaired, and it became a shelter for the homeless.

Finally, in 2010, the church was renovated once again. Much of the funding came from the Lutheran church in Bavaria. Now the beautiful building is the center of German life in Odesa and a global attraction.

If you count up all the years spent on the reconstruction and restoration of this church, it adds up to about *186 years*

The church was included as *an orientation poin*t on all sea maps because it was so tall and could easily be seen from the sea

53

One-Walled House

The so-called "House with One Wall" is, for obvious reasons, one of the most famous sights in Odesa's historic center

If you look at this building from a certain angle, it appears to have no side or back walls. In reality, the side wall was attached at a very acute angle, making it invisible from certain spots. The history of this triangular-shaped building is shrouded in speculation and legends, some mystical, but more of them simply absurd. Some sources say that at some point, the builders ran out of money and it became necessary to connect the two side walls and not build a fourth. Others believe that the original plans only contained three from the start due to a lack of funds. According to this version, the contractor slipped his drunken boss the plans, which he signed without examining. However, the layout of the apartments points to the fact that they were thoroughly planned and designed with precision.

In reality, the reason for designing such a non-traditional style of building is quite simple. The building is located

This building is known by several names such as "Flat House" and "House with One Wall," "House of Cards," "Witch House," and "House of Shadows"

in the heart of Odesa, on Vorontsovskyi Lane, but previously this was just a backyard street of Prymorskyi Boulevard. The street was quite narrow and due to the neighborhood's shape, and the lots were divided into trapezoidal, parallelogram, or triangular shapes.

The inconvenient shape of the lot was not at all a problem for its owner Heorhiy Rafalovych. In the late 1880s, the architect Telezhynskyi designed the large three-story house. Its construction was completed in 1889. There are actually several other irregularly shaped buildings in that area. In the Soviet period, the building suffered the fate of many other residential buildings the center of Odesa — it was divided into communal apartments.

Other "flat" houses in Odesa can be found on *no.12 Vira Inber*, *no.21 Lydersovskyi Bulvar*, *no.21 Stepova*, *no.3 Vera Kholodna Square*, and on *no.96 Bohdana Khmelnytskoho*

54

Moldavanka

Moldavanka's old courtyards with their numerous stone decorations, wooden porches, and gardens have stayed at the heart of Odesa

Moldavanka is a historic district of Odesa, associated gangster romance, which has existed since about the same time as Odesa itself or even earlier. There are no reliable sources to prove this, but information about a farm in this area first appeared in the years 1793-1794.

When Odesa obtained free port status, a flow of contraband was passed through Moldavanka. At that time the area was populated with all sorts of speculators, gangsters, merchants, and porters. All this made Moldavanka a dangerous but alluring separate world within the boundaries of Odesa. The unique setting and atmosphere were best described by Isaac Babel in his *Odessa Stories*.

One of the most famous legends of Moldavanka was of

In 1832, *the first hospital* in Odesa was established on Moldovanka's Miasoyidivska Street. The hospital was funded for a long time by Jewish families, so it is still referred to as the Jewish hospital. The hospital building was previously a manor estate, hence the unusual architecture for a medical establishment

the famous bandit and raider Mishka Yaponchik. Leonid Utyosov knew him personally, and Babel's character Benya Krik was based on him.

The origin of the district's name refers to the Moldovans who lived on the farm at the beginning of Odesa's history. But now this area is in no way connected to the people of Moldova. Besides the street name Tiraspol, a former road in Moldavanka, there is

nothing else which connects this area to the neighboring country.

A large inflow of money had little impact on the appearance of the buildings in Moldavanka. But the district is not renowned for its appearance. Instead, it is a place where you can still feel the subtle rhythm of Odesa. This is best characterized by the saying "Moldavanka is more Odesa than Odesa itself."

Most of the streets of old Moldavanka were laid with *cobblestones* imported from Italy. Many cobblestones were made from hardened lava from Vesuvius. In Soviet times, some of the cobblestones were paved over with asphalt

Starokinnyi Flea Market

Odesa's flea market reflects the essence of life in this city

Odesa's flea market is located in the center of Moldavanka, the former gangster area, and extends over several streets. The heart of the flea market is the Starokinnyi Rynok (Market) located in the area between Rozkydailivska Street, Skisna Street and Starokinnyi Provulok. But starting from Serova Street, there are tables with goods and antiques set up on the sidewalk. The flea market is quite difficult to navigate the first time you go there. However, those who make repeat visits will find that their legs will remember the way and lead them to where they need to go, be it the book area, dishes area or to the charming old ladies with their vintage clothes and accessories. Each seller has a fixed spot.

The Starokinnyi Market was first established in 1833, when it

In the days when animals were sold at this market, there were not only cows and horses, but also _____. After the Russo-Turkish war almost all the markets in the southern provinces of the Russian Empire were filled with them
A series of performances by "Art-raiders" was held at the flea market under the supervision of _____ _____. In them, artists created work from objects found at the flea market, and interacted with passers-by and sellers

was a place for buying and selling animals. Next to the flea market is a bird market, which also has thoroughbred puppies and kittens, as well as mixed breeds, which are often given away for free.

You can find almost anything at this flea market, from Soviet artifacts, like large crimson banners or huge canvas portraits of Soviet leaders, to the rarest editions of foreign books, to bicycles, drinking glasses of various shapes, musical instruments and antique furniture. Leaving the Starokinnyi Rynok with empty hands is next to impossible, particularly since most things there cost little more than a few pennies. And if you're lucky, you might get to enjoy a story or two from the people you buy from.

56

Monument to Esperanto founder

The only monument in Ukraine to the creator of Esperanto

At first glance, it seems logical that a monument to Ludwik Zamenhof, the founder of Esperanto, is located in Odesa, a city proud of its multiculturalism. However, it is not as simple as that — the monument was installed there by chance. Its creator, sculptor Nikolai Blazhkov, who was a follower of Esperanto, was commissioned to create the bust by a private customer. The order was carried out, but the customer did not appear. Therefore, Blazhkov placed the bust in the courtyard of his apartment on no.3 Derybasivska Street, where the monument is located to this day. At that time, Esperanto was forbidden by the Soviet government, so when questioned by the authorities, Blazhkov said it was a monument to his father. He told them he had placed it in the middle of the courtyard on top of the well so that hooligan boys didn't fall in. By the time the truth came out, the political climate had changed.

The monument was made out of plaster, and was restored by enthusiasts. However, in 2008, the local government decided to fund a professional restoration, in which the statue and well were coated with a marble-like substance.

As *a Tolstoyan*, Blazhkov preached non-resistance to evil, so did not take part in the Russian civil war. However, he was a soldier in World War II and spent time in both German and Soviet camps

Blazhkov and his students completed *a bas-relief of Maxim Gorky* on a wall of the Vorontsov Palace. Gorky was also interested in Esperanto

KREINTO
DE
ESPERANTO

Л.Л. ЗАМЕНГОФ.
АВТОР ЯЗЫКА
ЭСПЕРАНТО.
Скульптор Н.В. Блажков

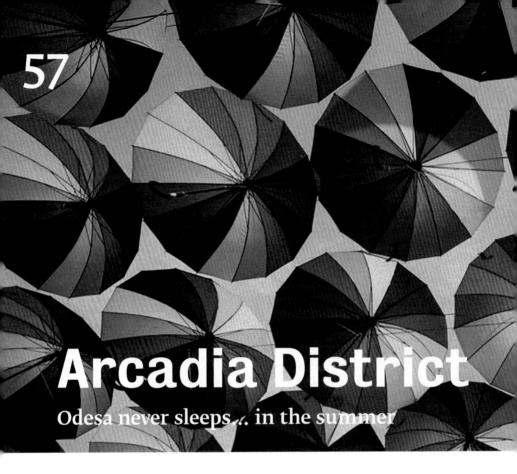

57

Arcadia District

Odesa never sleeps... in the summer

After recent renovations, Arcadia has turned into more of an open-air shopping and entertainment complex. There are many shops, cafes, restaurants and nightclubs, which is why this beach is more suited to those in search of a good nightlife scene. Odesa's loudest summer parties are held on Arcadia Beach.

Odesa is rightfully recognized as one of the best cities in Ukraine for nightlife. This is especially evident in summer, when it seems the whole coast and center of town don't sleep. You can spend the whole night going from one club to another, and finish off by watching the sunrise on the beach.

Much of the city's nightlife is centered around Arcadia. Over the past two decades, it has become a kind of cult venue. New clubs have opened, old ones have closed, or existing ones revamp themselves

For a few years there was a club called *21st century* in Odesa, which became legendary within a very short time frame. That did not save it, however, from eventual closure. The club remained empty for some time until eventually a Baptist church was set up there

Some clubs offer interesting additions to their basic services. Thus, in some you can get *a tattoo*, or in others, *a haircut*

or change their style. Two of the long-standing classic spots are the clubs Ibiza and Mantra.

The end of summer does not mean the end of the nightlife. Many Arcadia clubs and boardwalk areas have winter patios and residences.

Odesa also has several underground clubs, some of which have become legendary. One of them is the art museum of the club *Vykhid*, as well as the art club *Shkaf*. Though their best days have passed, Odesans still consider them cult spots.

In addition, there are closed raves at secret sites. Sometimes they are held on Kuyalnyk Estuary, sometimes in abandoned locations, and sometimes just on the street. Usually you can only find out information on them from the organizers themselves. However, you can usually find out where to go.

58

Karolino-Buhaz

The beaches here are the best of those along Odesa's coastline, and probably, in all of Ukraine

It would be difficult to come up with a better location for Karolino-Buhaz and the neighboring resort village of Zatoka. The large sandy area separating the Dniester Estuary from the Black Sea has its own unique microclimate. The 20km sand strip that is 50-800 meters wide has a vast number of recreation areas, sanatoriums and great beaches.

The Tatar settlement Boaz used to exist where Karolino-Buhaz now stands; it was destroyed during the Russo-Turkish war. Later the land was acquired by one noble family after another.

The best thing here is, of course, the beach. Almost 20 km long, it can rightly compete with Rio's Copacabana. Almost every

According to a widespread but erroneous story, the settlement originates from *Karolina Sobańska*, a famous adventurer and a woman to whom Alexander Pushkin and Adam Mickiewicz dedicated some of their poems. She married Odesa businessman Hieronim Sobanski. An alley was named after him in Odesa

The resort is located near the city of *BelhorodDnistrovskyi*, in which the famous Akkerman Fortress is located

Odesan knows that though the city beaches are good, if you want a really nice one, then it's best to go to the Karolino-Buhaz area. Here you can watch the sun rise above the sea and see it set over the estuary. And all this in an hour's drive by car, bus or train.

59

Zelenyi Teatr

This newly restored open air theater-park space continuously expands on its diverse program

The Zelenyi Teatr (Green Theater) in Shevchenko Park was the first open-air amphitheater in Odesa. In 1876, the Odesa City Council wanted to turn the area into a pond, resembling the outlines of the Black Sea. Unfortunately, (or perhaps fortunately), the municipal budget only had enough funds to dig a deep hole.

To prevent such a colorful place in the heart of the city from going to waste, port workers, fishermen from Langeron and nearby residents turned it into a huge football field. Incidentally, this is where the history of the famous Odesa Chornomorets football team began.

In the 1930s, city architects decided to turn the area into an amphitheater, opened on June 11, 1936. For many years it was considered one of the most visited and popular summer concert venues in Odesa.

In 2016, a group of volunteers set out to renovate the theater. Not so much with bricks and cement, but rather by incorporating modern ideas about a functional and relaxing city space. Renowned speakers, poets, artists, journalists and famous musical groups have already entertained audiences in the updated theater. There is also a space for showing new and retro films.

In Soviet times, artists such as **Edita Piekha and Sofia Rotaru**, performed here. In the '70s, people came here hoping to hear songs from **The Beatles, Deep Purple and Led Zeppelin**, performed by Polish and Czech bands. In August of 1996, the theater hosted the farewell concert of the legendary band **Nautilus Pompilius**

 2 Parkova doroga

NATURE

60

Black Sea

Odesa is inextricably linked with the Black Sea: since ancient times it has been an important transport and trade area

The Black Sea coast was colonized by the ancient Greeks, then the Romans, the Byzantines, the Slavic tribes, and the merchants of Venice and Genoa. Since then, the area has had a connection to the history and culture of those people.

It was in the Black Sea that Jason and his Argonauts searched for the Golden Fleece, and Hercules reached the Amazon by sailing across the Black Sea to perform his ninth feat. Remains of the ancient cities of antiquity can still be found

Among the planktonic algae that live in the Black Sea, there is a very unusual type, *the noctiluca scintillans*, or sea tinkle. It can exhibit bioluminescence, which can cause the Black Sea to glow at times in August

Top: Diogo Homem, **Portolan of the Black Sea,** *1559*
Left page: **Attic black figure neck amphora,** *530-520*

along the Black Sea coast. These remains provide a great opportunity to explore the history of the ancient world.

The Black Sea is a remnant of the ancient Tethys Ocean and has a very unusual feature. It contains a large amount of hydrogen sulfide, which makes the bottom layer unsuitable for living things. This is probably where the name came from. In the habitable areas of the sea, mullet, gobies, sprat, flounder, mussels and mollusks can all be found. They are all a part of Odesa's summer cuisine.

The mountains around the Black Sea continue to grow at a rate of a few centimeters per century, and the sea itself increases in size as well, at a much quicker rate of 20-25 centimeters per 100 years

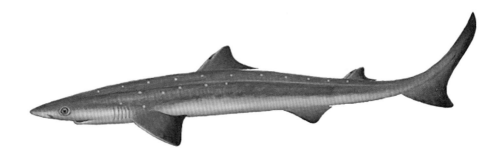

61

Spiny Dogfish

This Black Sea predator is completely harmless to humans

Who would have thought that you could encounter a shark on the Black Sea coast of the Odesa Gulf? Luckily, this type of shark is harmless. The spiny dogfish, or mud shark, does not attack people, preferring to go after sprats, gobies, and anchovies. With such a diet, it can be considered a real Odesan shark. After all,

these are all common in the diet of Odesans.

Spiny dogfish are also known as piked dogfish. They usually live near the coast, but they love cold water. Therefore, encountering a spiny dogfish at an Odesa beach during peak season is practically impossible. The best time for catching a dogfish is

In addition to spiny dogfish in the Black Sea, there is another type of shark which is much more rare — *the catshark*

The dimensions of this type of shark are even smaller, 60-70 cm in length, so they pose absolutely no danger to humans

This knife is also referred to as *"spiny dogfish"*, because of its form

considered spring and autumn as the water at this time is quite cool. Additionally, a lack of bathers on the beaches allows the fish to come very close to shore.

Spiny dogfish are a kind of trophy among fishermen and anyone who has caught one can be proud. One reason for this is that spiny dogfish are rare on the coast. The other is that they make excellent fillets. Knowing how to cook a spiny dogfish properly can turn an ordinary fisherman into one who possesses "secret knowledge." In addition, they get the pleasure of telling all the other fishermen the story of how they caught it.

62

No.20 Tram

Odesa has one of the top twelve most interesting tram systems in the world, according to Forbes magazine, along with those of Rio de Janeiro, Melbourne, and Lisbon

Almost all of Odesa's tram routes are interesting in their own way, and it is impossible not to notice the number of anecdotes and urban stories associated with them. However, one of the most interesting is considered to be the no.20 tram or, as some call it, the "Jungle Tram". This route connects the outskirts of the city center (Kherson Square) with Khadzhibey Estuary.

In the first few minutes of your journey you will notice the first feature, a complex web of paths, for which an arrow would be impossible to use. Such rail construction exists in only a

Trams are one of *the primary modes of transport* in Odesa. The tram network connects *the city center and industrial and residential districts*

Tram no.20 passes by *the* *"Bolshevik" factory*, which, among other things, is interesting for its inhabitants. During the construction of the factory, which began in 1911, *huge cicadas* were brought in, which somehow adapted to Odesa life and still live around the factory

few cities in the world. After the "Deaf Bridge," which was built especially for the tram, you will find yourself in industrial Odesa. You will see abandoned factories next to dilapidated houses, which, admittedly, have a certain charm. Then the tram leaves the industrial zone and takes Khadzhi-beiskyi Road, after which it passes a lake, which the locals refer to as Swan Lake. The tram then passes the

so-called cave houses (niches in the limestone, which had two exits, one onto the street and the other into cata-combs) where local bandits used to hide during raids. The next extraordinary sight the tram passes through are reeds, taller than the average person, from which the tram got its nickname. The end of the line is the Khadzhibey Estuary, an area of black mud that is said to have healing properties.

One of the main attractions of the route is *the Sotnykivska Sich Cemetery*, founded in 1775

63

Wild Beaches

While most people enjoy the comfort of a well-equipped beach, there will always be a certain charm in enjoying raw natural settings

In Odesa, a wild beach is considered one that has no sun chairs or showers and is usually deserted. In other words, human impact there is minimal. There are no such beaches left within Odesa's city limits, but outside of Odesa you can still find them. It is a great opportunity to be alone with the sea.

If you take the road out of Odesa toward Mykolaiv, you will get to the villages Fontanka or Nova Dofinovka, where you will find picturesque wild beaches with clay cliffs and huge blocks of yellow limestone. Although more people have found out about these beaches in recent years, there are still relatively few people

It's no secret that *Odesans like traveling out of the city to find a nice beach*. Some don't even bother looking; many residents of Odesa have been known not to set foot on the coast for the whole summer

here, and on weekdays, perhaps none at all. These beaches offer a beautiful view of the entire Gulf of Odesa, and the water is very clear, so you will have a good view of the ocean bottom unobstructed by algae or silt.

You can also check out a few beaches on the other side of Odesa, toward Bilhorod-Dnistrovskyi. The road you need to take passes through Sanzheika, Karolino-Buhaz and Zatoka. The infrastructure in this area is more developed, with resorts, hotels, and holiday cottages. However, you can also find deserted beaches with a wild coastline if that's what you're looking for.

It is best to look for one around Sanzheika, with its yellow rocky cliffs. Along the coast of the Gulf of Odesa you can always find an unknown beach or a small village. In most you can buy local wine for a pittance.

The sea absorbs more land each year along natural coastline that doesn't have breakwater, as it moves closer onto the rocks. Because of this, beaches and surf lines can *look different every year*, sometimes even beyond recognition

64

Ferry Swans

Only a short trip out of Odesa, a popular spot for swan watching can make an enjoyable outing for both tourists and locals

About twenty kilometers away from Odesa, near the Odesa-Chornomorsk ferry, is a popular spot for swan watching. For the past twenty years, swans have been spending their winters on the ferry. Gulls, ducks and other waterfowl can be found there too, but the swans are the most noticeable, because of their beauty.

There is *a small market* on the ferry, where you can buy fresh Black Sea mussels

Many birds fly to this ferry from the whole south of Ukraine and spend about six months there from October to March. They initially used the ferry as a stopover before flying to warmer climates, but over the years, they have felt so comfortable there that they remained on it for the whole winter. This is largely due to the fact that they had enough food to eat; the people coming to feed the beautiful birds often outnumber the swans themselves. The birds also look for food on their own. The Sukhyi Estuary rarely freezes, but on those rare days when it does, the port workers chop the ice for the birds. That way they can continue to eat their natural diet of beneficial foods, mainly eelgrass algae.

If you are interested in going to feed the swans, keep in mind that they are *hungriest in the morning*. If you don't make it out until the second half of the day, you'll need something more than ordinary bits of bread to attract their attention — for example, chopped vegetables or corn

65

Odesa's Cats

One of the best and prettiest of
Odesa's attractions

Nobody knows why there are so many cats in Odesa. You can see them walking down streets, or at home in various shops, theaters and offices. Entire prides have been known to inhabit apartment block courtyards. Some cats help to sell cigarettes and newspapers from kiosks, some live in the port and railway station, and others in hipster coffee shops. Even hairdressers practice their skills on their furry friends, when customers

Ukraine's oldestcat, *Veniamin de Lekli*, once saved his family from a fire, by calling attention to the flames with his loud meow

aren't around. You might even catch a glimpse of an Odesa granny in a gray robe and curlers feeding fried seafood to a cat at her window.

Almost certainly, the cats see themselves as full-fledged citizens of the city and treat people with a certain amount of skepticism.

Not surprisingly, there is a cat café in Odesa called Ko-teinaya, which houses 14 cats of different breeds and cross breeds. They include a Bengal cat, a Munchkin, and a Russian blue. All 14 of them have passports, are up to date with their immunizations, and are affectionate. They were all brought to the café from shelters with the help of volunteers. The cats can be stroked, squeezed, or even taken home to keep.

Almost all of Odesa's cats are very friendly and happy to approach people or pose for a photo; *some may even let you pick them up*

66

Sycamores

These are the greatest and most beautiful trees of Odesa

Sycamores and plane trees are not the same genus. Sycamores line Prymorskyi Boulevard, Katerynynska, Rishelievska and Pushkinska streets. They look especially nice on Pushkinska Street, where the overgrown branches of the trees planted on both sides of the street create a tunnel effect. Thanks to these trees, Pushkinska Street is almost always shady and cool on hot summer days.

It makes sense for there to be so many sycamores in Odesa, due to their high crown and bright

Ancient Greeks and Romans used to plant sycamores near their homes and temples. Despite their large size, Odesa's sycamores are still far from maturity. These trees can live up to *two thousand years*, and Odesa's sycamores are currently a mere two hundred years old

beautiful trunks. The shadow the sycamore creates is not as dense, for example, as that of the linden trees that grow on Derybasivska Street. Therefore, the sycamores provide cool shade but allow you to still enjoy the sunshine. When the city was first built, it was very hot and not very green, so these trees were much needed. Additionally, sycamores are incredibly beautiful, especially in the rain. When wet, the grayish bark darkens and takes on an emerald-green color.

67

Odesa Zoological Museum

Odesa is replete with museums and galleries, and there are even some exhibits hidden from the public eye

The Odesa University Zoological Museum was established in 1865 at the same time as the university itself. The original collection was previously located in the Natural History Room of the Richelieu Lyceum. In the Odesa University, however, this museum is part of the Faculty of Biology. The collection now comprises 56,000 artifacts, 7,500 of which remain on permanent display. The museum is currently used as an educational and scientific resource center for students and researchers. It occupies three exhibition halls comprising of a total area of 1,200 square meters.

The original collection was compiled by Alexander von Nordmann, a professor at the Richelieu Lyceum. He brought back from his expeditions a large selection of insects and skeletons from fossilized animals. Ilya Mechnikov, who the university

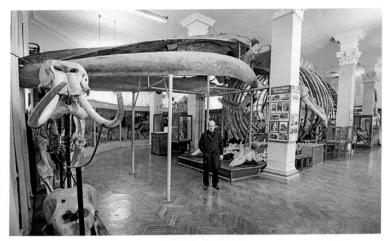

During *World War II* occupation of Odesa, the museum staff managed to save the most valuable artifacts. They immured them in niches in the corridors of the main university building located on Dvoryanskyi Street. Nevertheless, half of the exhibits were irretrievably lost

The most prized artifact of the collection is a valuable *29-meter skeleton of a blue whale*. It is mounted to the ceiling and can therefore be examined quite closely. The whale skeleton was given to the museum as a gift by the Slava whaling flotilla

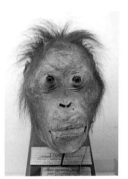

is named after, also made a significant contribution, including his collection of human skulls. The museum also houses stuffed mammals and exotic birds, fish, invertebrates, corals and much more, including rare artifacts.

The museum is very popular among students of the Faculty of Biology who go there in search of information for their projects and dissertations. Anyone is allowed to visit the museum, as long as they make an appointment in advance. The museum building is located on Shampanskyi Lane, and guided tours are held several times a week.

68

Kuyalnyk Estuary

There are seven estuaries in the vicinity of Odesa. Among them, the Kuyalnyk Estuary, known for its healing mud, stands out

The therapeutic properties of the Kuyalnyk Estuary's water and mud were first mentioned in 1829, back when it was called the Andriivskyi Estuary. Several years later, in 1833, Count Vorontsov ordered the construction of a hospital nearby. It was designed for taking mud, water and sand baths. It quickly became a popular healing spot. In 1842, a new sanatorium building was built to replace the old one, and roads leading up to the resort were paved. These roads greatly facilitated transportation to the estuary, which is located 12 miles away from Odesa.

Previously, it was also used as a major place for salt mining. After being cut off from the sea, Kuyalnyk's salinity increased rapidly. This estuary has been a famous place for salt mining since the Middle Ages. Wooden tools for the extraction of "white gold" have been preserved on the beaches. Today, Kuyalnyk Estuary is so shallow that in some places you can walk across it. Each autumn the water and the sand on the bank acquire a blood-red hue due to the algae rotting away, making this area look like a martian landscape.

The Kuyalnyk spa and health resort is considered the oldest mud health resort in Ukraine. Besides the mud, which is considered the main treasure of the estuary, the mineral water "Kuyalnik" was once bottled there. At one time it was supplied to the court of Catherine II

On the banks of the estuary, the remains of ancient settlements can be found, including those of the Scythians. Traces of a settlement were also found on Zhevakhova mountain, which is adjacent to the estuary. Remains of dishes and and utensils dating back to between the sixth and second centuries BC were found

SPORTS

*Right page: Ihor Belanov hangs **the Golden Ball**, 1987*

69

Serhiy Utochkin

He was a great dreamer and an "academic" athlete. Serhiy Utochkin was also the second person in the Russian Empire to fly a plane

He was a test pilot, an aviator, a boxer, a cyclist, a motorcycle racer, a yachtsman, a football player and a swordsman, and he achieved success in almost every sport. He achieved 14 wins in international and national cycling, won the Odesa championships in fencing and tennis, swimming and wrestling. In addition to his athletic success, Utochkin was known for his unusual and often comical antics. He was the first person from Odesa to ride down the famous Potemkin Stairs on a bicycle. He later repeated the trick both on a motorcycle and in a car.

In 1907, Utoch-
kin made *a hot
air balloon
flight over the
Egyptian pyr-
amids in Gaza.*
It was just two
months after his
first flight

Utochkin was a
member of the
Odesa British
Athletic Club and
was one of the
first people in the
Russian Empire to

become involved
in football. Prior
to this, football
matches were
mainly played
by foreigners,
particularly

British players.
Serhiy founded
*two football
clubs* in Odesa
and became the
chairman of one
of them period

*The
Chornomorets
Club* was later
formed on the
basis of the
British Althletic
Club

However, Utochkin's greatest passion was for aviation. A few months after his first flight in a hot air balloon over his native Odesa, he flew over the Egyptian pyramids in an air balloon. After this trip, Serhiy made his first flight on a biplane and became the first aviator from Odesa.

There is a monument to Serhiy Utochkin in his native Odesa, in the heart of the Odesa City garden. There used to be a cinema on that spot, which was named in his honor while he was still living.

70

The Health Road

The Health Road is a coastal pedestrian and cycle road, connecting Odesa's beaches from Langeron to Arcadia

This well-known road for health enthusiasts was given its name after it became popularly used for various sports. The five-kilometer roadway along the sea was originally built as a bypass, but quickly became a very convenient place for walking and other sports. Both adults and children alike come here to run, cycle or rollerblade. Along the coast you can find outdoor gyms and playgrounds, both older Soviet and newer ones. You can also find cycle tracks for fans of extreme cycling. A nice amble along the Health Road allows you to enjoy the sea breeze and spectacular views.

Most people start out at Langeron Beach, which you can get to from Shevchenko Park by going through a beautiful arch that was once the

While the movement of cars or motorbikes on the Health Road is prohibited, it was originally designed as *an emergency or detour route*

main entrance to the cottage of Governor-General Count Langeron. Slightly below that you will see the Dolphinarium and the new boardwalk, which marks the starting point of the Health Road.

Continue along the road for about two kilometers and you will end up at Vidrada Beach. Along the way you will see a few wild beaches. A reference point for many generations has been and remains a large yellow rock. Back in the days before mobile phones, couples would often use the yellow rock as a meeting place for dates.

Odesa's famous cable car also passes over the Health Road. In just five minutes it will take you from Frantsuzkyi Boulevard right to the beach. The final destination is Arcadia Beach, well known for its nightlife and beaches.

The Health Road periodically serves as an a venue for a variety of *cross-country competitions*. In addition, in recent years, it has been used for the initial section of the Odesa 100 ultramarathon

71

Chornomorets

The game of football appeared in Odesa in the second half of the 19th century, where it was brought by the British

The first football club in Odesa was founded in 1878. It is notable that it delegated players to the Odesa league team that won the Russian Empire Championship in 1913.

The history of the Chornomorets football club began in 1936 under the name Dynamo Odesa. After changing names several times, the club has remained the Chornomorets since 1958. The club's first major achievement was winning the USSR championship in 1961. In the 1974 season, Chornomorets returned to the top division of Soviet football, and immediately became the bronze medalist of the USSR championship. The Odesa club became the first to win a national championship in the newly independent Ukraine in 1992 and repeated this achievement in the following year.

The Chornomorets Stadium was considered as one of the host stadiums for the *2012 European Football Championship*

Internationally, notable matches included those against Werder Bremen, Lazio Rome and Real Madrid. Also memorable was the victory over the only winner of the Champions League, the Red Star from Serbia, and an away game win over repeated champion PSV Eindhoven.

The club is closely linked with the names of a few famous players. These include Ihor Belanov, who received the Ballon d'Or in 1986, and Viktor Prokopenko, who led Chornomorets to success in 1992-1993. A symbolic club of Ukrainian players who have scored over 100 career goals has been set up, named in honor of Tamerlan Huseynov. Since 2013, the club has been playing in the new arena with a capacity of thirty four thousand spectators, which is located in a scenic park overlooking the sea and the port.

The first game of the Ukrainian Super Cup was held at Chornomorets Stadium in 2004

72

Ihor Belanov

Ihor Belanov went from playing football
in his apartment courtyard to being named
the best football player in Europe

Belanov started his football career
with SKA Odesa, then transferred
to Chornomorets Odesa. Due to his
mastery of techniques, powerful
sprint and accurate shots he was invited to play on both the USSR Olympic team and Dynamo Kyiv. While
playing with Dynamo, he won two
USSR championships and the Cup
Winners' Cup of 1986. That was also
when he received his major individual football award, the Ballon d'Or.
In 1987, he was invited to play with
the symbolic team of FIFA, and a
year later he took part in the match
against the French team while
wearing the World Team's jersey.

After playing for Dynamo,
Belanov transferred to Borussia
Mönchengladbach and then to

Belanov was the only player from the USSR who was able to score *three goals* in one match at a World Cup. He accomplished his hat trick in a match against Belgium in *the 1986 World Cup in Mexico*. However, even his outstanding performance did not save the Soviet team from defeat, with a score of 3-4

Ihor Belanov is one of three Ukrainian players to have received *the Ballon d'Or*. Another recipient was Oleh Blokhin, one of his Dynamo Kyiv teammates, and Andriy Shevchenko, striker for "Milan" and the best scorer of the national team of Ukraine

Eintracht Braunschweig. When he returned to Ukraine, he briefly played again for Odesa's Chornomorets, but soon after retired.

Ihor Belanov was honored with one of twelve commemorative stars on the Chornomorets football Walk of Fame, established in 2012 in front of the football stadium in Taras Shevchenko Park.

After retirement Belanov opened a football school in Odesa, which carries his name.

73

Odesa 100-km Ultramarathon

This is a traditional cross-country running competition that even Olympic athletes would find challenging

Every year, a running ultramarathon called the Odesa 100 (Odeska Sotka) takes place in April. The 100-km track passes through places of World War II military glory; the competition appeared in the mid-1970's as a tribute to those who fought for the liberation of Odesa from Nazi forces. A 24-hour time limit is placed on the race, during which runners have to complete the 100-km track with several checkpoints along the way. Anyone is allowed to participate. The diverse competitors can be seen at the start of the race, when athletes and physical education students are lined up beside pensioners and schoolchildren. Incidentally, one of the oldest and most regular participants is over 80 years old.

In earlier times, the signal to start the race was made by a real cannon Sometimes it happened without warning, which made the event especially memorable

Left page: The starting point of the **100-km Ultramarathon**

In the last 10 years, a 100-km race has been added for cyclists. It's part of the same competition, but "only" 10 hours are allotted for cyclists to finish the race. The vast majority of cyclists complete the race in 5-6 hours. It is considered much easier than the running race. Many participants arrive on unusual bikes such as tandems, one-, three-, four-wheeled bikes, recumbent bikes and even circus bikes. Some people even try to do the 100km on rollerblades or longboards.

In addition to cycling and jogging, there is also an Iron Man competition. It is similar to other Iron Man competitions, in which participants cycle to the end of the track and make the return journey on foot. The purpose of the competition is not to complete it within a certain time frame, but to challenge oneself.

74

Chess Players

On Soborna Square near the monument
to Prince Vorontsov there is a gazebo where
you will hardly ever find an empty seat

Many generations of Odesans have gathered here to play chess, checkers, backgammon or cards. Originally, the gazebo was used as a meeting place for football fans to discuss the latest matches, players and coaches. Discussions on politics, sports, and other hot topics have remained constant, although the format has changed in many ways.

Usually, chess matches are played for a monetary prize or bet on, but money is never put on the table, and keeping track of amounts owed is done in code. This often works against players, because the sophisticated codes are easily forgotten. Sometimes it is difficult to remember who owes whom and how much. The audience also place bets, and usually one of the spec-

Recently, one of the communal utility works installed *electricity* so that chess matches could continue after sunset

Sam Kislin, one of the richest people in the USA, once *played chess* in the Odesa gazebo. Born in Odesa, where he worked as deputy director of the central department store, he moved to the USA in the 1970s. He founded the Trans Commodities company and became the *first honorary citizen* of New York to be born outside the United States

tators is chosen as a judge — for a small fee, of course.

There is an urban legend about the actions of two con artists in the 1980s. They were considered average chess players but suddenly began to play like real chessmasters. The onlookers began to take bets, and the prize at stake was huge for the time, 200 rubles. They played all day and late into the evening. The au-

dience even recorded their moves. The game ended late at night, when they had no choice but to call it a draw, which allowed them to split the money. Then they got up from the table without even collecting the chess pieces. Apparently, they were never seen in Odesa again.

TECHNOLOGY

Right page: The probability of a particle with an energy of E overcoming the barrier (the Gamov factor)

$$\Gamma(E) = \exp \left\{ -\frac{4\pi}{h} \int_{x_1}^{x_2} \sqrt{2m[U(x) - E]}\, dx \right\}$$

75

Port of Odesa

Ukraine's largest port and major transportation hub

Odesa's Port was established on the same day as the founding of the city itself, September 2, 1794. It was that day that the first posts were driven into the Velykyi and Malyi (Big and Small) piers. The head of the port was Odesa's first mayor, José de Ribas. The port's porto franco/free port status, assigned in 1819, had a significant impact on its development. The Odesa harbor quickly became the second largest in terms of cargo turnover in the Russian Empire after St. Petersburg. At the end of the 19th century, the port's cargo turnover grew to double that of St. Petersburg.

The development of the port led to the construction of the Potemkin Steps, which connect the city of Odesa to its harbour below, and are considered an entrance to the

The Odesa port was the base of the Black Sea Shipping Company. **It was founded in 1863** and was the oldest on the Black Sea. In addition, the Black Sea Shipping

Company was *the largest in Europe in terms of number of vessels.* After the collapse of the USSR, the company went bankrupt and all the ships were sold

There is also *an oil and gas terminal* at the Port of Odesa. The terminal is the biggest one in Ukraine; it has six berths with a total storage capacity of *671,000 m³*

city from the port. The red brick warehouses in Karantynna port became its symbol, along with the Vorontsov Lighthouse.

During the Crimean War, the port was bombed by a Franco-British squadron. In commemoration of this, a rifle from the *Tiger* frigate warship, which sank near the harbor, was installed near City Hall. The port also played a key role during World War II, as it was a strategic site from which people could evacuate the city.

When Ukraine became independent, the port of Odesa became the largest cargo handling and passenger traffic port in the country. Each year, the largest passenger liners in the world enter the Odesa marina.

Ilya Mechnikov

He was a Nobel Prize laureate
in the field of physiology and medicine

Ilya Mechnikov is considered one of the most important scientists in the field of evolutionary embryology and immunology. He was born in the Kharkiv region in 1845 into a noble family. His talents emerged at an early age, and in the 6th grade he independently translated a French book on physics.

    He completed a four-year degree in two years and graduated from Kharkiv University in 1864. After graduation, he continued his studies in Europe. In Naples, he met biologist Alexander Kovalevsky. Together they made discoveries in embryology. After defending his doctoral dissertation in 1867, he became a professor at St. Petersburg University.

Ilya Mechnikov tried to commit suicide *twice*, both times due to his marriage. His first wife was ill with tuberculosis and Mechnikov tried unsuccessfully to find a way to cure her. When she died, after only 4 years of marriage, *the scientist drank a large portion of morphine*

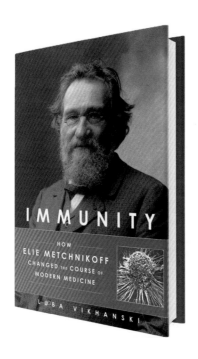

At the age of 22 he moved to Odesa and taught at the local university. He worked there as a zoology professor and lecturer for 12 years. In 1886, Odesa's mayor Hryhoriy Marazli used his personal funds to establish a bacteriological institute, which was the second in the world after Louis Pasteur's institute in Paris. Under the leadership of Ilya Mechnikov, vaccines were developed for use against various diseases.

In 1887, he was invited by Louis Pasteur to work at his institute in Paris. In 1908, he received the Nobel Prize for his work on human immunity.

However, he vomited the solution and was spared from death. His second marriage, too, was in trouble when his wife became ill with typhoid fever. Mechnikov injected typhoid bacteria into his own body in order to die with her. Fortunately, *he and his wife both recovered*

Yosyp Tymchenko

Two years before the Lumière brothers created the first motion picture camera, Tymchenko had created his own version in Odesa

Yosyp Tymchenko was born in 1852 in Kharkiv province to a peasant family. While living in Kharkiv, he became inspired by the ideas of Miklukho-Maclay and decided to take a trip to Oceania together with his friends. However, the group of travelers split up in Odesa, and Tymchenko stayed on to work in the shipyard. In 1880, he was hired to work as a mechanic at Odesa University and was put in charge of the mechanical workshop.

It was there that Tymchenko invented his motion picture apparatus. It was an intermittent mechanism, which allowed the user to intermittently change frames in a stroboscope. From this he invented a kinetoscope, and recorded images on a photo plate. With the help of this device, he screened the first two films the world had ever seen, *The Javelin Thrower* and *The Galloping Horseman*. The films and kinetoscope were demonstrated in Moscow, but were not properly appreciated. In the meantime, the Lumière brothers created and patented their device, the cinematograph.

IIn 1875, Tymchenko designed *an electric watch* while working in the shipyard. It was first presented to the governor of Odesa, and then sent as a gift to the emperor of the Russian Empire, Alexander II. However, the watch was lost along the way

Tymchenko was an across-the-board inventor. Among his inventions was equipment for the hospital located at the Kuyalnyk Estuary. He also invented *microsurgical instruments for eye operations, a number of meteorological instruments, and a mechanical telescope device for tracking the orbit of the planets*, which was made for the Odesa Observatory

78

Krayan

This former train car repair workshop has now become a place of industrial tourism

In 1863, a railway workshop complex was built in the developing Odesa. The construction of the workshop buildings was initiated by Baron Karl von Ungern-Sternberg. After his death, city architect Arkadiy Todorov significantly refurbished and extended the project.

The monumental red brick building has been one of the best examples of industrial architecture of the 19th century. The most important building of the complex is the main locomotive shop.

In 1994–1995, the enterprise employed about *5,000 people*; in 2000, the staff was *1,303 people*, and as of January 1, 2001 — *1,262 people*

During WWII, *the NOR-1 tank* was designed on the complex. The design was based on a tractor, which was trimmed with sheets of steel. The tank was not particularly effective, but the noise it made was frightening

After Ukraine gained independence, the complex was shut down. The buildings gradually deteriorated from fires and weather conditions.

In recent years, the complex has become a place of interest for stalkers and city explorers. It is a great place to explore due to its convenient location, unguarded area, and the interesting remains of 19th-century architecture. It is located near the train station, not far from the city center. The red brick buildings of the former complex stand out clearly against the backdrop of gray industrial zones.

October 12, 2015, the inactive one-story carpentry workshop built in 1902 was completely *destroyed in a fire*

79

Vladimir Filatov

"Every person should see the sun" — the motto
of the great ophthalmologist Filatov

Vladimir Filatov came from a noble family of physicians. His
uncle was the founder of Russian pediatrics, and his father
specialized in ophthalmology. He received a good education,
and it was expected he would continue with the family tradition of pursuing a career in medicine.

After moving from his native Simbirsk to Moscow, he
entered the faculty of medicine at Moscow State University.
After graduation he was invited to work as an intern at Odesa
University, and ended up spending the rest of his life there.

In 1921, Filatov began working as a professor at the university. In 1936, he purchased a plot of land with his personal
funds, on which he established the Odesa Institute of Exper-

Filatov's approach
with patients was
also unique. After
the operation he
would personally
accompany his
patients to the
beach. There he
would remove
the bandages
so the first thing
his patients saw
was *the sea and
the sun*

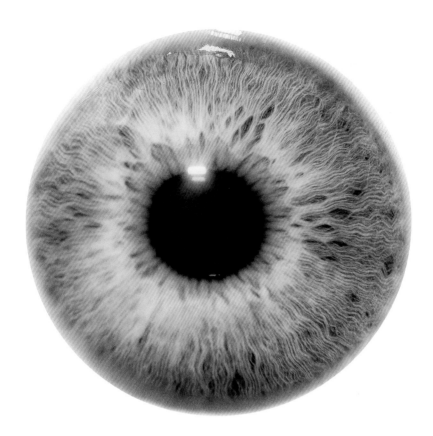

imental Ophthalmology, which later became the the Filatov Institute of Eye Diseases and Tissue Therapy. Filatov served as director of the institute until his death, and it was there that he made all his discoveries. One of the most significant was a new corneal transplant method. This made the previously complicated procedure available to any qualified ophthalmologist.

In addition to his work at the institute, Vladimir Filatov taught for seven years at a specialized school and founded his own ophthalmologic school. His approach to teaching allowed for the widespread use of innovative therapies.

An asteroid discovered in 1982 was named in honour of Filatov. It is noteworthy that it was discovered by the same astronomer as Gamov's asteroid

80

George Gamov

The famous scientist was one of the developers of the Big Bang theory

George Gamov (Georgiy Gamov) was born in Odesa in 1904. His mother was a history and geography teacher, and his father was a Russian teacher. His parents were well respected in the city and taught at the best schools. They encouraged the young Georgiy to study the exact sciences. After graduating from high school he entered the Physics and Mathematics Department of Odesa University. During his studies he worked part time at the Odesa Observatory.

In 1922, he was transferred to Leningrad University due to reforms in the education system. After finishing graduate school he created the theory of alpha decay. While working on this

A few objects in space are named after Gamov. These include *a crater on the back side of the moon, named in his honour in 1970, and an asteroid, identified in 1984*

$$\Gamma(E) = \exp\left\{-\frac{4\pi}{h}\int_{x_1}^{x_2}\sqrt{2m[U(x)-E]}\,dx\right\}$$

The probability of a particle with an
energy of E overcoming
the barrier (the Gamov Factor)

theory, Georgiy met with the creators of quantum physics, Max Born and Niels Bohr.

In 1933, Gamov emigrated to America with his family, where he became known as George Gamov. He worked as a professor at George Washington University where he made a number of discoveries in the fields of nuclear physics. One of the most important of his works is the Big Bang theory. Initially, this theory was not widely recognized, but with time it became commonly accepted. In addition, Gamov made an unexpected contribution to microbiology when he developed the theory of the genetic code.

All three of Gamov's fundamental discoveries served as the basis for further research in these areas and have brought the Nobel Prize to those who made later contributions.

Gamov helped to make science popular. In 1938, he wrote *a science fiction story about the adventures of* **Mr. Tompkins**, first published in **Discovery** *magazine*. In 1940, he published a collection of short stories. The collection has been reprinted several times and translated into many languages